ESSAYS ON THE
DEPOPULATION OF MELANESIA

ESSAYS
ON THE DEPOPULATION
OF MELANESIA

EDITED BY

W. H. R. RIVERS, M.D., F.R.S.
FELLOW OF ST JOHN'S COLLEGE, CAMBRIDGE

WITH A PREFACE BY

SIR EVERARD IM THURN, K.C.M.G., K.B.E., C.B.

CAMBRIDGE
AT THE UNIVERSITY PRESS
1922

CAMBRIDGE
UNIVERSITY PRESS

University Printing House, Cambridge CB2 8BS, United Kingdom

Cambridge University Press is part of the University of Cambridge.

It furthers the University's mission by disseminating knowledge in the pursuit of
education, learning and research at the highest international levels of excellence.

www.cambridge.org
Information on this title: www.cambridge.org/9781107511903

© Cambridge University Press 1922

First published 1922
First paperback edition 2015

A catalogue record for this publication is available from the British Library

ISBN 978-1-107-51190-3 Paperback

PREFACE

I GLADLY accepted an invitation to contribute a preface to this collection of essays dealing with a specific case of the inter-relations of white men and "natives," a subject which for fifty years has been of the greatest interest to me, and one which, if till recently it attracted less general interest, has now become of very great and ever increasing imperial importance. The British nation has, almost unintentionally, assumed more or less control over a very great part of the tropical lands, the former occupants of which were folk who, at the time when their home-lands were first entered by people from the West, were in a state of culture, primitive indeed but often very complex, and so entirely different from that under which our own social system has developed as to be, at first sight, almost unintelligible to us. In the past a few of us have partly understood the obligation, but as a nation, we are only now fully realising that, in assuming control of these lands, we have saddled ourselves with the duty of providing as well as may be for the welfare and comfort of the earlier occupants; and still more are we only now realising that, in order adequately to fulfil this duty, it is necessary, as a preliminary, to get understanding not merely of the physical requirements but, at least as much, of the ideas and feelings of these folk of culture quite different from ours.

The essays on the "Depopulation of Melanesia" which follow seem extraordinarily well suited to focus the attention of all thoughtful people on the problems thus presented to us, and, perhaps more clearly than has before been done, on the causes of failure in the past—sadly indicated by the dying out of the people, as also to suggest more or less possible ways of even now remedying the mistakes of the past, with due regard to the interests of those Europeans who have settled in the islands under consideration, and have there acquired substantial interests.

It is a happy chance that the regions dealt with—the chain formed by the New Hebrides with the Santa Cruz and Solomon Islands—were the latest to be invaded by European settlers, so that there the Melanesian folk retained till a much later date, and in almost absolute purity, their own ideas, customs and culture generally, whereas in Fiji and the more easterly islands the record was blurred at an earlier time by the intrusion, first of European waifs and strays, next by the earliest missionaries, and even by actual settlers.

It is also fortunate that the authors of these essays, writing, it may be observed, independently, are exceptionally well qualified, by personal experience, to deal with the matter from several different points of view. The three missionaries who have contributed have all worked in one or other of the islands under consideration, and, in varying degree, each has tempered missionary zeal of the old fashioned kind and his sympathy with the natives of whom he took charge by a wise application of anthropological lore and methods. Dr Speiser, on the other hand, having gone to the islands to study the folk from the point of view of a scientific anthropologist, has evidently, during his two years of wandering through the various islands, acquired, if indeed he did not already possess, that sympathy with the folk whom he was studying which the old fashioned anthropologist sometimes lacked. Mr Woodford, to whom more than anyone else the present development of the Solomon Islands is due, and the late Sir William Macgregor, whose experience of administration over similar folk was exceptional, have

PREFACE

written as administrators, but without letting their natural
zeal for the European development of the islands interfere
with their interest in, and sympathy with, the islanders.
Lastly the editor, one of the most acute of present-day
anthropologists and psychologists, after spending much time
in eagerly, and most sympathetically, studying the islanders
in their homes, has contributed the final essay, in which,
after justly appreciating the facts recorded and the theories
put forward by the other writers, he suggests definitely, and
almost convincingly that, without at all under-estimating
the destructive effect on the islanders' race of physical ill-
treatment, sometimes deliberately but much more often
quite unintentionally inflicted on it by Europeans, the true,
that is to say the most potent, cause of the decay of the race
is the loss of interest in life which they have suffered owing
to the change which we have brought about in their surround-
ing conditions—perhaps unavoidably but certainly without
fully appreciating the effect of what we were doing.

The history of the European invasion of the Solomon
Islands and the New Hebrides, so far—and it is of course
very far—as this has been responsible for the present condition of the islanders, may usefully be briefly recalled. The
islands in question lie outside and south of the one main
track, ordained by the winds and currents, which was
habitually followed by European ships for some centuries
after the first discovery of the Pacific Ocean; and, except
for the brief, almost momentary, Spanish attempts at
colonising—by Mendana, in 1567, in the Solomon Islands,
and by Quiros, in 1606, in the New Hebrides—and for the
still more brief visit of Tasman's ships in 1643, through
those seas, there is hardly any record of intercourse by
Westerners with the islanders till towards the end of the
eighteenth century. Doubtless some of the ships that passed

that way, driven by stress of weather to an unknown end on some undiscovered island, may have scattered a few white men among the folk already in occupation of those parts, and that, in such cases, these "lost explorers of the Pacific," as Sir Basil Thomson has called them, may to some slight extent have influenced the arts and ideas of the primitive folk among whom they had been cast away. But any such influence must have been very transitory, for few, if any, traces of it have been noted. It was not till well on in the nineteenth century, when first the sandalwooders (about 1840) and, a very little later, the earliest missionaries established themselves in the New Hebrides, that any considerable European influence was brought to bear on the islanders of those parts. This influence was carried further northward along the group by the many Frenchmen who, after New Caledonia was taken possession of by the French, in 1853, as a convict station, strayed thence into the islands. Still further north, in the Solomon Islands, there does not appear to have been much, if any, European influence till a little later, until indeed the Melanesian Mission, between 1853 and 1856, extended its work to those parts, though not long after this settlers began to scatter themselves over these islands also.

It is not difficult to understand that the few Europeans who thus settled in islands into which white men had hardly before ventured, and where consequently the natives had retained their customs, ideas, and manner of life to a degree rarely seen elsewhere, found the difficulty of establishing even the most necessary intercourse between the intruders and the islanders was very great indeed. It was all the greater in that the white men were divided among themselves; the missionaries and the traders were more or less opposed to each other, and bore themselves towards the natives in very different ways.

The trader, whose main purpose was to get from the islander all that he could, in the way of produce, land and labour, found that he could best get this by treating such of the natives as could supply his wants in these respects with sufficient, if sometimes delusive, kindness and justice, and that he had no occasion to interfere further than this with his Melanesian neighbours' ways, customs and interests. The missionary, on the other hand, saw before him as his one main task the very difficult duty of persuading as many as possible of the islanders suddenly to throw aside practically the whole of the habit of thought and action which, followed through an untold number of generations, had made them, and their forefathers, contented and, in their way, happy, and in place of all this as suddenly to take on the entirely different and infinitely more elaborate habit of thought and deed which has made the people of the western world what they are. It was certainly a stupendous task, especially as the earlier missionaries had no authority to back them, except such as they could assume for themselves; and great credit is due to them for having effected the conversion, even if at times this was of a somewhat artificial nature, of so many of the islanders.

One regrettable effect of this earlier form of missionary effort, well-intended as it was, has been the partial obliteration of the record which might have been obtained of the islanders' habits of thought. Not many years ago, in a tiny and little visited New Hebridean islet, where, however, there has for some time been a mission station, it was my fortune to step over the low dyke of loose stones, exactly such as in those parts is used to keep the too numerous pigs out of the dwelling-houses, and was told that in this case it separated the mission quarters from those of the so-called "heathen"; within the pale, the houses of the Christian occupants were comparatively clean, and the people themselves were in European clothes, of a dirty but not extravagant nature. The missionary was away at the time; only a few yards outside the pale, I passed, rather unexpectedly, on to the dancing-place of the heathen—as weirdly interesting a scene as one could see. The place was almost surrounded by huge old fig trees, their gnarled branches, some of these dead and leafless, showing out like witches' claws against the sky: in a circle, half buried among the fantastically growing aerial roots of these, were a number of shrine-like erections, each surmounted by a huge figure of a bird, its wooden wings lifted straight up till they touched the overhanging branches of the trees; within each shrine was a great stone, the purpose of which was betrayed by the special wooden club, for the ceremonial killing of pigs, which had been left resting against some of the stones; and here and there in this welter of survivals from an old and little known stage of culture were long table-like stages built of bows, and laden with row upon row of the New Hebridean's greatest treasures—pig's lower jaws, the tusks of which had been caused to grow almost incredibly long, till some of them had formed one or even two complete circles. Here and there, too, there were life-sized figures of men made, after the characteristic style of New Hebridean art, of some soft dark wood, patterned with stripes of red, yellow, and white. It was on one of these human figures that there was the most surprising of all the things seen on that day; for from where the waist should have been, if the lower part of the figure had been more than very roughly worked out—there hung what was quite clearly meant to represent a crucifix, such as the image-maker had doubtless seen carried by the Fathers from the Roman Catholic Mission on an adjoining island.

The things seen on this island suggested perhaps more vividly than anything else could have done the almost immeasurable difference between Melanesian and European cultures, and the sharpness of the line which still divides them where they come in contact.

Almost simultaneously with the earliest settlement of Europeans within these Melanesian islands, Europeans of another kind appeared there from time to time, to disturb the peaceful lives not only of the islanders but also of the missionaries and settlers. The "labour traffic" had been begun about 1847, when Pacific Islanders were successfully imported into Australia for work on the sheep-runs. At first the labourers thus taken were chiefly Polynesians from the Gilbert Islands and other islands still more to the east; but the increasing demand from Australia, and subsequently from Fiji, for labourers of this sort caused the recruiters to turn their attention to the Melanesian islands. There is no occasion here to dwell on the brutality and disregard of the interests and rights of the labourers with which this trade, at times certainly, was carried on; but, as a rule, when the men were once at work on plantations they were not badly treated, and in a sense they even benefited, by introduction to habits of steady labour. Naturally, however, the settlers in the Melanesian islands resented the depletion of their labour supply; and, still more frequently, the missionaries resented the frequent removal of members of their flocks.

But the worst result of this labour traffic was in the effect that it often, though not always, had on the characters of the islanders who were the subjects of it. Far away from their own islands, and surrounded by men who had no interest in them except as labour-machines, they too often picked up the white man's vices without any of his good qualities; and, even if they were fortunate enough to be sent back to their homes at no very long time after they were due for return, they were apt to carry with them either bitter resentment against the white man or keen longing to get back to the more exciting experiences they had had in the white man's country. Nor, greatly changed as they generally had been by these experiences, were they always very welcome at home. Even their own folk, to whom they must have seemed as men returned from the dead, hardly knew or wanted them; and the missionaries, who, by the seventies, about which time the labour trade had entered its worst phase, had built up for themselves a sort of theocratic government, more or less recognised or at least respected and feared by the islanders who had stayed at home, but not at all by the returned wanderers, found themselves thwarted at every turn by certain of the last named. It is but fair to add that some of these returned islanders—those who had been fortunately treated during their service abroad—became useful members of society in the islands to which they returned, though others became in the highest degree dangerous to the peace and welfare of that society, especially by stirring up hostility to the Europeans.

The state of unrest in these Melanesian islands eventually became so serious that, in 1873, the first step was taken to supplement and back the necessarily weak authority which the few and scattered resident missionaries had contrived to assume. The first "Pacific Islanders' Protection Act" was passed in the Imperial Parliament in that year; and two years later—Fiji having at that time acquired the status of a Crown Colony—the opportunity was taken to strengthen the Act by the appointment of a High Commissioner for the Western Pacific, with instructions and authority, within such of the islands as were not subject to any Foreign Power, to protect the islanders against aggression by British subjects, and, incidentally, to protect Europeans from attack by the islanders, but without power to intervene in disputes in which natives alone were concerned.

These first steps were in the right direction; but to give effect to them it was obviously necessary to provide the High Commissioner, who was resident in Fiji and could not even visit the islands at frequent intervals, with assistants to reside and carry out the scheme in the islands. At first this assistance was limited to a single Deputy to reside in each of the main groups and the occasional assistance of a Naval Captain, who was deputed to visit the islands from time to time—during such season of the year as was not subject to hurricanes! Considerable additions, it need hardly be said, have since been made to this totally inadequate staff, but even now the number of Government representatives resident in the islands throughout the year is quite inadequate to enforce British law and justice throughout this chain of widely scattered islands.

A further remedial measure, for the special purpose of checking the misdeeds of certain of the labour recruiters whose activities had by that time earned the ill-name of "black-birding," was taken. Immigration Agents were appointed by the Governments of Australia and Fiji, to control the business, and each labour vessel proceeding to the islands was accompanied by a special "government agent," whose business it was to see that no islanders were recruited against their will and that all who were taken received fair treatment during transport. By these means great improvement was certainly effected in the way in which the trade was carried on; that the old evils were not completely cured was due chiefly to two facts, partly that it was impossible to stop recruiting from islands so remote as to be practically beyond the ken of the few Europeans resident in the groups, and partly that the recruits from the islands, however humanely they might be dealt with, could not but suffer in character by removal from their island-homes, where, indeed, their innate ideas and customs were but little understood by the few Europeans with whom they there came in contact, to entirely new surroundings where it scarcely occurred to any one to try to understand and make allowance for the mental attitude of these labourers of strangely primitive culture.

Now that the labour trade, even under its improved conditions, has been, though only quite recently, entirely prohibited, it is useless to deplore but useful to bear in mind the evil consequences which it has had on the Melanesian character.

Meanwhile, settlement by Europeans on the islands proceeded, with varying success, one result of which was to bring very difficult "native land questions" into prominence, and with the general result that some form of actual annexation by a Power able to enforce its regulations became essential, in the interest both of the islanders and of the European settlers.

In the case of the Solomon Islands, annexation by Great Britain, though it was effected somewhat late in the day, was comparatively easy; for, with the exception of the large northernmost island of Bougainville, with one or two small islands close to it, the whole of the group had for some time been undisputedly under British influence. It was unfortunately otherwise in the case of the New Hebrides, where, French and British interests being quite inextricably intermingled, the best that could be done was to patch up an Anglo-French "Condominium," which novel and remarkable political experiment, even though it might be effective as regards purely European interests, is entirely inadequate, owing to the radical difference between British and French views in such matters, for the control and help of the islanders.

To sum up: it can hardly be doubted, and least by those who read these essays, that the rapid disappearance of the Melanesian folk of these islands is a direct, however unintended, consequence of the settlement among them of Europeans; and it seems almost as certain that while this calamity is due, certainly in great measure to the action, often necessary and, under the circumstances, unavoidable but sometimes also callous and even brutal, of those who have gone there for the immediate purpose of developing and exploiting the land, it is also due in some measure to the well-intended, but sometimes mistaken and ill-calculated, and sometimes inadequate, efforts of missionaries and Government representatives to save the islanders from the worst effects brought on them by the in-rush of Europeans.

The facts put forward by the essayists suffice at least to indicate the nature of the causes which have brought about such deplorable effects. Briefly put, and always allowing for the too frequent cases which there have been of actual inhuman treatment of the islanders, the main cause of whatever failure there has been in the efforts of those whose desire and duty has been to soften the impact between the two races that have now met in the islands has been want of understanding by us of the islanders and failure to grasp the immense difference which lay between their culture and ours. Settlers, missionaries, and Government representatives have all, in varying degree, been hampered by this form of error.

Comparatively minor instances of the ill-effects of this fundamental mistake are put forward by the various writers in this book; and Dr Rivers, in the final essay, has focussed attention on the one which is perhaps the one chief ill-effect of all—we have, quite unintentionally no doubt, destroyed the islanders' interest in life. The earlier missionaries, always, it must fully be admitted, suppressed, probably they seldom succeeded in destroying, the islander's instincts and ideas corresponding to our religion, and imposed upon him instead our own utterly different ideas of that sort; they first also persuaded the islander of the righteousness of clothing his body, with the result, of course afterwards fostered by the traders, that he developed a taste for unbecoming and utterly insanitary European clothing. Meanwhile, the settlers deprived the islanders of much of their best land and its produce, thereby depriving them of another of their occupations and interests. And, at a somewhat later time, Government stepped in and found it necessary to suppress such of the islanders' customs as were entirely inconsistent with the safety of the mixed human society which had come together in the islands—with the result, often quite unintended, that the islander got the idea that he could practise only surreptitiously such of his habits and customs as were not after the European fashion; moreover, the deprivation of the really obnoxious customs from which he was necessarily prohibited, such as head-hunting, was a really serious loss to him, for head-hunting had been not only an interesting sport but his one means of proving his manhood and gaining his wife. And even the kinds of illness and disease to which he and his forefathers had been subject were revolutionised by the introduction of European diseases. It was indeed a changed world in which the islander found himself—and one in which he had little desire to stay.

It is difficult to see clearly what remedies should now be applied to this obviously evil state of affairs. Certain remedies are tentatively and somewhat hesitatingly indicated in these essays, and with most of these suggestions I agree. But, even after having thought over the matter for years, it is only with diffidence that I offer some suggestion on this difficult problem.

There can be no possible doubt that the most essential step, even at this late date, should be the systematic study, by all Europeans resident in those islands and charged with, or interested in, the welfare of the natives, of the habits, customs, and ideas natural to the Melanesian; and here it should be remembered that, owing to the historical circumstances above recalled, the Solomon Islanders, and to a less extent this is true also of the New Hebrideans, have, behind the veneer of doubtfully genuine European culture which has been imposed on many of them, retained much of their own culture and social organisation, so that even now it is easier to get at their own original ideas and feelings than it is to ascertain the unadulterated feelings and ideas of the Fijians or those of the natives of other Pacific Islands which for a longer time have been centres of European life.

Secondly, the best way to treat the natives having been ascertained by the above-mentioned means, there should be greater co-operation—indeed it should be as complete as possible—between the Government representatives and the missionaries in systematically carrying out the treatment thus determined on. The number of missionaries scattered through the islands and in intimate relations with the island folk is not great; and the number of Government representatives correspondingly situated is still less. Economy, no doubt, prohibits any great increase in these numbers. Co-operation between Church and State, if it were possible in any way to bring this about—say to the extent that the resident missionaries' services might be enlisted as Justices of the Peace—might help considerably toward better care for the physical welfare and mental interests of the Islanders.

In this, as in so many other matters tending toward better administration in the islands, the difficulty would probably be less in the Solomon Islands than in the New Hebrides, owing to the existence in the last-named group of the Condominium and the greatly different views of the French and British Governments as to the treatment of natives.

EVERARD IM THURN.

23 *April*, 1922.

CONTENTS

I

INTRODUCTION

THE event which led to the production of this volume was the receipt by the English representatives of the Melanesian Mission of the first two articles in this book. One of these came from the Rev. W. J. Durrad who had served for many years in the Mission, chiefly in the Torres and Banks Islands. The other was a report written by Dr Felix Speiser of Basle, which had been translated by the Rev. A. I. Hopkins, a member of the Melanesian Mission. Dr Speiser had spent two years in Melanesia, chiefly in the New Hebrides, and had published many of his observations in a book which appeared in 1913 under the title *Two Years with the Natives in the Western Pacific*. In the paper which comes next to that of Mr Durrad he has put on record his impressions concerning the depopulation of Melanesia and the measures by which he believes that it may be arrested.

Towards the end of the war it was suggested that these two papers should be published and it was felt that their value would be enhanced if other members of the Melanesian Mission would also place on record their views concerning the problems raised by Mr Durrad and Dr Speiser. Reports are here published from the Rev. A. I. Hopkins who is working in the Solomons, and from the Rev. W. C. O'Ferrall who is especially acquainted with the Santa Cruz Islands. Mr C. M. Woodford, who was for many years Resident Commissioner in the British Solomon Islands, has also been good enough to record his views and a letter written in response to an inquiry, by Sir William Macgregor, not long before his death, has also been included in the volume. Lastly, a paper dealing especially with the psychological causes of the dying out of the Melanesian people has been written by the editor, this paper embodying experience gained during visits to the Solomon Islands and the New Hebrides in 1908 and 1914.

Dr Speiser's paper was written as long ago as 1912 and other papers are already several years old, so that they may not portray the present state of Melanesia exactly. There is little doubt, however, that any change has not been in the direction of improvement. Each paper expresses only the opinion of its writer. Neither the editor nor the Melanesian Mission must be taken to accept the remedies and solutions suggested in individual essays.

The part of the world of which the volume treats is one of peculiar charm and interest. The islands which make up the Melanesian archipelago, and lie along the western borders of the Pacific Ocean, are little known and until fifty years ago were but little touched by outside influence. They do not lie on any important trade-route, such as those which have led to the great development of the Hawaiian Islands or Fiji, while the jungle-covered islands and the fierce hostility of many of the inhabitants placed obstacles in the way of commercial development. But though this development has begun late, there are few parts of the world where it has had so destructive an effect upon the native culture and upon the welfare of the people. The chief purpose of this volume is to call attention to the approaching extinction of a picturesque people and to put forward suggestions for measures by which they may not only be preserved, but be enabled to take their part in making the fertility of their islands of use to their fellow-men.

II

THE DEPOPULATION OF MELANESIA

By the Rev. W. J. Durrad

IT is a great satisfaction to learn that there are people in England who are troubled about the decrease of the population of Melanesia, and I gladly avail myself of the opportunity which has been given me to foster that feeling of concern, for if we could get a sufficient number of persons of influence to know and care about the rapid diminution of the Melanesians some steps might be taken to retard that decrease or even to turn the scale the other way. It is not impossible, and it is not yet too late to save them. But it soon will be. This is as certain as anything can be.

That the people are decreasing and decreasing fast is well known. Articles in the *Southern Cross Log*[1] dealing with the work of men in their districts allude from time to time to the evidence of a large population that existed in former days. And anyone who has spent a few years in Melanesia will have noticed, between the time of his arrival and that of his departure, a distinct difference in the number of people among whom he has lived. The longer his stay extends, the more marked becomes the fall in the population. Whether the people had begun to decline before the advent of the European is unknown. Personally I should say there was no decline, but rather a tendency the other way. I say a *tendency* only. That the islands were not overstocked was the result of heathen customs which kept the population down. I allude to fighting, infanticide, infant mortality,

---

[1] The monthly journal of the Melanesian Mission.

malignant magic which had tremendous effect, neglect of useless and infirm people, and the extermination of those whose conduct put them outside the pale of morality. For we know quite well that heathen people have a very strict moral code of their own as to what is and what is not permissible. All these forces acting together kept the population more or less at the same level. Decrease in population began with the advent of the European. I do not say the missionary. Probably the old sandal-wood traders started the process.

Introduction of diseases. This is undoubted. Disease resulting from immoral life was probably unknown before the white man came. It exists now but not probably to a great extent. Whether the effect of this disease is seen in children who are subject to almost perpetual running sores I cannot say. A few boys at my school are badly developed and are scarred with the marks of old sores on legs, body, neck, and arms, which need only a knock to become large ulcers which take weeks to heal. This is surely unnatural and points to some constitutional defect. Well fed and cared for as they are, they should not naturally be liable to such outbreaks.

Dysentery was probably known in former times as there is a native word describing the phenomena connected with the disease. But whether it ever assumed the violent form which it has done in recent years it is impossible to say. It seems to occur in very dry seasons. But such times of drought are rare as the rainfall in these islands is very large. There is no proper dry season. A year or two ago there was a long spell of dry weather and there was an epidemic of dysentery throughout all the Solomons which carried off great numbers. The disease was probably carried by trading ships.

Measles is rarely seen, though a few years ago there was

an epidemic in Raga (Pentecost Island in the New Hebrides). This must have been brought by some vessel.

But the diseases which are decimating the people are pulmonary. On asking a trader in Santa Cruz as to the cause of the decrease in the number of people there, a decrease so evident in the smaller and smaller number of canoes which each year put out to meet the 'Southern Cross[1],' he told me that great numbers died of chest complaints. I am not speaking of consumption, which was well known to the natives in their former state of isolation. For that complaint there is a native name and it carried off a certain number of young people. The chief present scourges are bad colds developing into bronchitis or pneumonia and these are brought from outside. Common colds are worse for Melanesians than for us and more likely to lead to bronchitis. It has to be confessed that the 'Southern Cross' is one of the chief agents in the distribution of pneumonia germs. This was noticed long ago by the natives. The following extracts read in the light of long personal experience are charged with a terrible meaning. Writing in June 1861 of a boat journey Bishop Patteson says:

"By 4 or 5 p.m. I neared Aruas, in the bay on the west side of Vanua Lava.... Somehow I did not much like the manner of some of the people; they did not at night come into the men's common eating and sleeping house, as before, and I overheard some few remarks which I did not quite like— something about the unusual sickness being connected with this new teaching."

Again in August 1863, in summing up a voyage he speaks of landing a party of his scholars on Mota where he "found them all pretty well." He went off for a trip to the south. He continues,

[1] The vessel of the Melanesian Mission.

"In another fortnight I was again at Mota. I found things lamentably changed. A great mortality was going on, dysentery and great prostration of strength from severe influenza. About twenty-five adults were dead already.... I spent two days and a half going about the island.... During these days twenty-seven adults died, fifty-two in all, and many, many more were dying, emaciated, coughing, fainting."

Who brought the influenza here spoken of? It is obvious that it was the Mission party from New Zealand, coming from that country in the winter when colds are rife, and the same thing happens now. Among the many occasions I can recall of severe illness following the ship's visit none stands out so prominently in my memory as an epidemic of pneumonia that raged on Ticopia when I was put down there on one occasion for a few weeks while the 'Southern Cross' cruised among the Solomons. What should have been one of the happiest of experiences was converted into one of the most tragic. The message of the Gospel was stultified by the terrible sufferings of the people. Forty persons, most of them in the prime of life and many of them fathers and mothers of large families of children, were struck down in death. Others, though very ill, survived, but were reduced to the condition of living skeletons.

Concerning the liability of natives to contract white men's complaints, Bishop Wilson told me he had consulted Sir Patrick Manson on the subject. The doctor pooh-poohed the seriousness of the fact and said that the thing happens all over the world and that the natives simply have to get inured to the new conditions. The tragedy is that in the process of becoming inured the Melanesians are becoming extinct. We are carrying on in the twentieth century what Dean Inge describes as a mark of the nineteenth. "The European races established their ascendency over the whole

planet, introducing the blessings of civilisation to the savage
peoples whom they exterminated" (*The Church and the Age*).
Introduction of alien social customs. The use of alcohol is
fortunately localised. But readers of the Annual Report of
the Mission, especially the article on Omba (Lepers' Island)
written a few years back by Mr Grunling, will be familiar
with the horrible conditions which prevail there. The existence of the sale of alcohol is well known, but owing to the
difficulties connected with the dual control of the group,
apparently nothing can be done.

Of all the evil customs introduced by civilisation the
wearing of clothes is probably the greatest. The Melanesians
are ignorant of the real objects of clothing and seem to look
on it more as a way of ornamenting the person than as
anything else. Of the three objects of clothes—the covering
of indecency, the retention of warmth and the exclusion of
cold—they understand the first. But so do many heathen,
for islands are not lacking where some sort of clothing which
is entirely adequate is worn. Those islands are indeed fortunate where, as in Santa Cruz and the Reef Islands and
Ticopia, the people make their own clothes, the men wearing
a loin-cloth and the women a modest skirt. These people
need nothing else. And where calico is required owing to
the absence of the home-made article, the very scantiest
supply is amply sufficient. European clothes are unnecessary
and are a source of disease. Moreover they are worn without
any system of consistency. A man will wear, perhaps, a
flimsy loin-cloth and a hat. Another day, a warmer one,
he may appear in a shirt in addition. On yet another occasion one sees him in a pair of trousers only. Or again in
trousers and waistcoat. Or, if a full blooded indentured
workman, he appears garbed in trousers, shirt, possibly also
a vest, a dungaree jacket and a hat. Most of the children

in the Banks Islands seem to wear a singlet in various stages of preservation. The singlet is worn till it is a mere network of rags. The women wear several layers of skirts and often a sort of short bodice. As a skirt becomes ragged another is superimposed, while the rags beneath gradually rot off. Clothes are worn till they cease to exist as recognisable garments. In a climate such as that which prevails here on Vanua Lava the custom is disastrous. The rainfall is abnormally heavy, the average being half an inch a day all the year round. The gardens are situated in the bush miles from the villages and one constantly sees processions of men, women and children going by with saturated clothes clinging clammily to their limbs. This would not matter much if the wearers changed completely when they reached home. But they do not all do so. They will sit and dry themselves at a fire. For a person in the prime of life and in the pink of health this would not be so serious, but it is disastrous for those who fall victims to influenza colds and coughs, and yet have to go out to collect their daily food.

The Melanesian Mission has not been and still is not guiltless of fostering this evil custom. When we read Bishop Patteson's life we see how abhorrent to his mind were European clothes for natives, but the circumstances of the work compelled him to introduce their use and we read how he himself rigged his scholars in shirts and trousers when on their way to Kohimarama[1]. The fact that the Mission worked there and at Norfolk Island in a subtropical climate necessitated the wearing of a good deal of clothing. The continuation of the Norfolk Island school helped to a certain degree to retain in the native mind the association of European clothes with Christianity. In the islands there is no need for such clothing, yet it is worn a good deal by all our

[1] The early school of the Melanesian Mission in New Zealand.

teachers, and clothes of some sort or other form an item in their stipends. Individual missionaries have been guilty of strengthening the desire for European clothes, and I have heard of a teacher being rebuked for wearing only a loin-cloth when coming to interview the missionary.

In our Mission native women, with the exception of girls trained at Norfolk Island, do not wear the full dresses such as are sold by store-keepers and provided for women on plantations. They wear a skirt and a separate bodice. The skirt alone is, to my thinking, quite enough and provides the maximum of decency and the minimum of risk. When travelling through our diocese a few years ago, a doctor expressed some strong criticisms on the over-dressed state of the native girls who had been trained at Norfolk Island. Most women who have attended sewing classes are appa-rently shy of being seen without jackets on. It is a false modesty. We have to rid ourselves of the idea that clothes make for a higher morality. It is by no means so. A Raga woman in an abbreviated mat skirt of native make is every bit as moral as a Banks Island woman with a bodice and a long skirt reaching to the ankles. Some of the most prudish women are not renowned for a very virtuous life.

In the encouragement of the wearing of clothes we are not the only offenders. The Presbyterian missionaries with far less excuse (for their own work has been from the beginning carried out altogether in the tropics) have taught their con-verts to dress in European clothes. But they are less in favour of this than formerly. Whilst staying at a Presby-terian Institution recently, I heard the Head express his pleasure at finding that some of the young men at the school were beginning to abandon their shirts during work-time in the gardens. He was not in favour of European clothing but he could not change the rule of the school. The Committee who managed the affairs of the Mission decreed that every native man at the Institution should be provided with three suits of clothes a year. The Church of Christ, a recent development in the islands of the New Hebrides in which the Melanesian Mission works, *i.e.* Pentecost, Omba, and Maewo, are the worst offenders of all. They teach their adherents that no one can be a Christian who does not wear shirt and trousers, and I have heard of their converts actually expressing contempt for our people who were clad only in a scanty loin-cloth. Perhaps longer experience may be modifying their opinions and teaching.

In the matter of clothes, the Condominium Government has given a bad lead. One of the regulations is that an employer of labour must provide each of his workmen with two or three (I forget the exact number) suits of clothes a year. This leads to the prevailing idea among the natives that they must wear clothes if they are hired to work. So it comes about that if I hire a few young men from the neighbouring village, they will march up on a sweltering midsummer morning in January or February, clad in hats, trousers, shirts, possibly vests, and coats. The sweat and discomfort produced by this "get up" must be very exhausting, to say nothing of its unsanitariness.

Prohibition of heathen customs. As one finds that the decrease of the population is not confined to Christian islands, it proves that the prohibition of heathen customs by missionaries or governments does not produce it. I used to think that the introduction of Christianity had some effect in lowering the vitality of the people by making life less strenuous, but I am inclined to modify this view. For a less strenuous life, a life where the struggle for existence was not so fierce, would not result in an immediate and rapid decrease. It would be a long drawn out process and not observable for some years. I do not say that the prohibition of heathen customs has not *some* effect. A great deal of satisfaction has been felt by government authorities in the Solomons at the abolition of head-hunting expeditions. True, it was time they came to an end, but the government when it took away at a stroke the chief occupation of the men, viz. war and preparation for war, put nothing in its place, and now I have heard from a traveller in the Western Solomons that the men simply loaf about and smoke in idleness. A government edict that extinguishes war is not going, *ipso facto*, to convert a savage warrior into a peaceful agri-culturalist. In this case there is probably experienced a great loss of vitality and zest of life.

When one thinks of the prohibition of heathen customs, one naturally first thinks of fighting as being the most anti-Christian of acts. War is carried on among heathen in a treacherous way, though it behoves Europeans in these days to criticise very gently the so-called barbarism of savage fighting. The heathen man has certain ideas of honour and right. When his pigs are shot, or his women-folk interfered with, or the right to his land is disputed, he also, as well as his civilised brother, will up and smite the offender. The fact remains that constant fighting did nothing to ex-tinguish the race. These Melanesians throve for hundreds of years in spite of the barbarities of warfare. It is, I believe, a recognised fact that during wars and pestilences, the birth-rate goes up, Nature making good, as it were, for the wastage of life. In times of peace which now prevail we may expect to find a lower birth-rate.

In certain directions in the sphere of morals heathen society was more strict than present day custom. Re-striction of excesses was then, of course, a matter of external order and not, as Christian teaching endeavours to make it, a thing of inward righteous feeling. For a time at least, Christianity tends to loosen the bonds of restraint, for it removes the terror of the punishment that would have been meted out by the chiefs of former days. An incestuous person, for instance, who outraged the native moral code, would have been shot or otherwise despatched, but now he is still left to follow his evil ways and no punishment follows. Missionaries can wield only spiritual weapons and when these are unheeded nothing can be done. Governments refuse to interfere in internal social affairs. They neither know nor attempt to know anything of them. It is only when a white man is killed that a government official starts reprisals. Now-a-days there may perhaps be more loose living than formerly on the part of young men and women. In heathen times the old men, being polygamists, claimed most of the women for themselves and guarded them with jealous watchfulness. There was not the freedom for promiscuity which is possible now. Whether promiscuity has or has not an injurious effect on the birth-rate is a matter for doctors to decide.

There is no doubt that social life as a whole is a more drab affair now than it used to be. But where Christian influence and teaching are strong there is provided a compensating interest and stimulus which outweigh the loss of old customs. But it is, to my mind, a matter of debate how much of the old order should be prohibited where it is not possible to give Christianity in its fulness. To send a badly equipped teacher to a heathen place to exercise a merely negative and repressive influence is of doubtful value. When his scanty message is exhausted, there follows a condition of stagnation and lifelessness which is neither heathenism nor Christianity.

Recruiting. This has from the beginning been a great source of depopulation. The facts relating to the Queensland traffic of former times are so well known that they need not be dwelt on here. But it is necessary to state the case as things now stand. The Queensland traffic is a thing of the past, but recruiting still goes on to supply the various French and English planters with native labour. I am speaking only of South Melanesia. The regulations drawn up by the French and British governments differ chiefly in this, that whereas British recruiters may not engage female labour to be ordinary plantation workers, the French are allowed to do so. Female labourers, according to British regulations, are allowed, I believe, to be engaged for domestic service under certain restrictions. However, the broad difference is that British planters may not recruit women, and French planters may. This causes great bitterness among the British. So much so that there is a very strong desire among them for the islands to be altogether under French jurisdiction. Also they seem to feel that they are allowed no voice in the government of the islands, whereas the protests and petitions of Frenchmen receive a sympathetic hearing. They also have a firm belief that the Presbyterian missionaries have, through the Scotch members of Parliament, a great power in exercising pressure upon the British Resident to restrict their freedom. Many of the British planters deliberately disregard the rule forbidding the employment of women workers on their estates. They do not recruit them in the ordinary sense of the term, that is, they do not make them "sign on" while the recruiting vessel lies off the island from which the women come. They accept them as "passengers" to their plantations. The women of course want to go. They are not forced. Frenchmen at times use violence and craft to get recruits but I have not heard of an Englishman doing so, at least not of late years. The British Government is stricter in enforcing discipline than the French, though the British of recent years have been slack enough. When I tackled the manager of a trading company on Vanua Lava, on the subject of the rule with regard to female labour, he told me he did not consider he was doing a wrong thing in employing women on his plantation. On his plantation are a large number of Torres Islanders. In fact, the Torres Islands are his chief recruiting ground and he has had for several years almost a monopoly of the place. He is a very kind man, scrupulously just and upright, and is much liked by the natives. He has a number of young unmarried women on the plantation, girls from Loh and Toga. He told me that he allowed no interference with these women by the men and punished without mercy anyone found molesting them. He confessed he did not do this on religious grounds, of which he disclaimed all profession, but simply to avoid the "rows" which follow a mixture of men and women. But he seemed entirely blind to the fact that he was helping to exterminate the Torres people. He, like all planters, wants strong young people, so he takes as many as will come to him. Among these are a number of young women who have no business to be working on a plantation at all, and least of all as unmarried women. They ought to be at home bearing children. But traders do not look at the future. In the general scramble for dividends, the great questions of the years to come are disregarded. The Torres Group is particularly in need of every individual native that belongs to it, for the decrease of the population has of late years been more and more rapid. Mr Jacomb in his book *England and France in the New Hebrides* (a book which ought to be read by those interested in Melanesia) makes a special point of urging the temporary prohibition of all recruiting from that group for a term of years to give the people a chance of recovering from the losses they have sustained. In many ways the Vanua Lava plantation is the best the Torres people could go to. It is near and the company's launch runs to and fro, so that they are in touch with home. They are given no alcohol and are repatriated immediately their term expires. How different it is with those who are enticed further afield to plantations in the Southern New Hebrides! Numbers of Torres people have gone never to return. Kept in debt by their French masters or tempted by alcohol, they are tied and bound for term after term of service and can rarely get free from the bonds which hold them. The 'Southern Cross' has often brought back to the Torres men and women from Vila who have escaped their life of indentured labour, yet have looked in vain for a means of returning to their home. It is pitiful that such a condition of things can continue without any attempt at redress or reform from year's end to year's end.

Infant mortality. This is very great, and, judging by the conditions of native life, probably has been so always. In heathen times, in addition to the ordinary ills that infant flesh is heir to, we have to reckon with the practice of infanticide that prevailed. The custom accounted for many deaths. It is, so far as we know, not practised now, at least not openly. There is no open throwing of an unwelcome baby to the sharks as in old days. Abortion is and always was practised and unfortunately is not regarded as a great crime. It is not considered on a par with infanticide. It is not reckoned as anything approaching the crime of murder. Considering everything the birth-rate seems to be distinctly good. A large number of babies are born and most of them are splendid specimens and often continue to remain so for several months. The midwifery is sufficiently good and the people consider there is very little risk connected with childbirth except in the case of first-born children. Deaths in childbirth are very few. The method of feeding new-born children is crude and stupid. The mother's milk is supplemented from the earliest moment with chewed taro or yam. This practice is followed in spite of all entreaties, suggestions, upbraidings and advice on the part of European missionaries. The village dames gather round the newly born and the old time-honoured custom is followed. "*We* were brought up like that," is their defence, and it is impossible to convince a tough old hag that her method of child-rearing is wrong. She considers herself a living witness to its excellence. There must be some injury to the digestive organs of the tiny infants, one would think. Some no doubt die of dyspepsia coupled with other ills. Only the very toughest can survive. So it has been always, only the strongest living, the weaklings perishing. It is really surprising that any survive at all. Infected with malaria as they are from their first entry into the world, living in smoky huts, irregularly washed, subject to curious eruptions and itching inflammations, there is yet found a certain proportion of children who attain maturity. With proper care many would no doubt survive that now succumb in the struggle to live. One is justified in believing that if all the babies born were to grow up, these islands, instead of becoming more and more a wilderness, would soon be thickly populated. Since August 1906 to the present date there have been about 145 infants baptised here at the school. They belong to villages within ordinary walking distance. This number does not represent the complete birth-rate, as some children are not brought at all and others die in the first day or two after birth. I do not think that the clerical baptisms of infants have ever been entered in the register. Of these 145 children, 66 are now dead. The head teacher of the biggest village near here has had six children but only two are now living.

What has been said of the evils of clothing applies to a certain extent to the babies. They are always carried either in the arms or astride on the hip or in a carrying scarf and come in contact with any clothing the parent happens to be wearing. The children have to be taken out in all weathers, for there is no nursemaid to relieve the parents and no *crèche* to consign the baby to while they go out to work. Food has to be got and the gardens, situated miles away, must be visited and the baby must go too. A leaf of the umbrella fern gives some, but imperfect, protection from the rain. I know no spectacle more wretched than to see a tiny child, covered with sores and whimpering with misery and discomfort, being carried on a soaking wet day on the back of a woman whose garments are a sodden mass.

The stamina of natives. We have been accustomed, for I do not know how long, to say that the Melanesians are not constitutionally strong. I use the phrase myself without knowing exactly what I mean. If it is meant that the vital energy of a Melanesian is deficient, then we are wrong in using the term, for what I have said about the ability of children to survive the horrors of babyhood proves surely that these people are possessed of strength and vitality beyond mere muscularity. The truth seems to be that the "make up" of a Melanesian differs in some subtle way from that of a European. It is hard to explain how. One realises the difference after living in contact with them without being able to explain exactly what one feels. There is a fatalism in their outlook which reacts upon their physical organism. While some complaints, such as a bad ulcer, which would prostrate a European at once and possibly kill him, will be patiently, stoically, and even cheerfully borne and even not interfere very seriously with the activity of the patient, a man will succumb at once to what appears a trifling indisposition. No native will be cheerful in illness or make any attempt to look on the bright side of things. I have never recognised any instance of what is known among us as the will to live when ordinary human judgment would pronounce death inevitable. An utter depression and abandonment of all idea of fighting an illness takes possession of a sick Melanesian. They may perhaps suffer in ways that medical science has not yet discovered. Dr Rivers, after staying in Simbo in the Western Solomons, told me that he found the natives often subject to mysterious swellings which he could not diagnose. Perhaps post-mortem examinations might tell us a good deal about the maladies they suffer from. As it is, many deaths that take place seem mysteriously sudden and inexplicable. No doubt many deaths occur owing to the total ignorance of scientific nursing. Again and again in seeing a sick person in a hut, one feels that, given proper care, he would certainly recover and live to enjoy many years of life.

Physically the natives are very strong and in spite of the rather exhausting nature of the climate are capable of tremendous exertion. It often surprises me to see a schoolboy here shoulder a great rough log and carry it a long distance apparently without any great strain. A European boy of the same age and size would probably not do it as easily. And when interested in work or stimulated and excited to exert themselves they can keep on at very heavy labour for a long time without feeling exhausted. It seems to be a habit of some people to describe Melanesians as lazy. Experience has led me to feel that a Melanesian's manner of working is the only possible one if one is to live for any length of time in these islands. The European comes vigorous from a childhood and youth spent in a cool climate to live a life of great energy and unceasing activity for a comparatively short time in the tropics. The natives with their slowness and habit of interspersing bouts of work with long spaces of rest irritate him. From what I have seen of some planters who looked for full value for their money, I should say there was a risk of native labourers on their estates being worked too hard. To start at daybreak and work till nearly sunset with only a two hours' break at midday is too much if it is to be continued day after day. I have seen natives under some masters looking thin and exhausted from the prolonged strain. It is possibly this that has made it more rare now than formerly for a native to "sign on" to work for a term of three years as was formerly the case. Now-a-days natives prefer as a rule to look to a local planter for a job. They will engage to work for even so short a time as a month. Curiously enough, the short term man is paid nearly double the money earned by a long service man. Natives prefer piece-work rather than working by the clock, if, of course, the section marked out by the master is not unreasonably large. Working with excitement at high pressure they finish the task before the ordinary "knock off" time and enjoy the extra rest. Where natives work by the clock, a gang is superintended by what is known as a "boss boy." He receives larger wages but does no work, his duty simply being to sit by and keep watch against slacking. It was where this system was in vogue that I noticed the exhaustion of the workers. The system of working might very well be a subject of enquiry by the Government.

Melanesian women as well as the men are physically very strong. I have seen a girl of Hiw in the Torres Islands carry a very heavy box balanced on her head for a distance of two miles along rough uneven paths and rocky coast. Women even more than the men are the survival of the fittest, for no man will marry anyone incapable of working. A girl with a physical weakness will remain unwanted. One would find no chivalrous youth marrying a weak girl to whom he would devote his strength and help. Such romance is not to be found in Melanesia.

It is probable that the stamina of the people is suffering already to a slight extent and will suffer more and more in the future with increasing rapidity in just such proportion as the population decreases. For with the decrease in numbers there will arise the inevitable tendency to close intermarriage. Natives do not care to go far afield for wives and it is even with dislike that they tolerate marriage with people of a neighbouring village.

Unsanitary modes of living. The modes of life remain the same as of old, while the conditions of life, so to speak, are changing. The manner of living needs change to suit the changing conditions. A hut buried in the bush, overshadowed by trees, and surrounded in wet weather by a quagmire was all very well in heathen times. The introduction of clothing is one of the chief reasons why such a condition of life is no longer sanitary. Also with each generation there steals over the community a subtle apathy. There is no need in these days for the intense alertness which was necessary in heathen times if life was to be preserved. One notices that when people become Christians they do not, as a general rule, get up so early in the morning. The softer modes of life need a better environment to counteract their enervating influence. There is need for large clearings round houses and villages so that the sunshine can come in and the air circulate. Some school villages are fairly good in this matter. I do not think the people need better houses. A well built house in the Banks or Torres Islands is really quite an excellent domicile, especially when built as some are, in generous proportions, high and strong. Where the ground slopes much, as in some Banks Island villages, platforms of earth and stones are built up with considerable labour and the houses on such places are as dry as the proverbial bone.

The food also is good and very well cooked. The Banks

Islanders are, as a whole, very big eaters. They would not be contented with what would satisfy a Raga or a Torres man. The people may be considered practically vegetarians as they eat pork only rarely and as a luxury. Perhaps a more generous diet of meat might help them to make a better stand against the various ills which are now brought into Melanesia. I do not think the tinned meat and so-called "salmon" do them much good. They indulge in these at times when they have money enough.

The people are exposed to infection by mosquitoes. It is a good regulation of the Government that compels traders to provide mosquito nets for their workmen. Natives look upon a net only as a means of getting peaceful sleep. What they are told by Europeans with regard to the Anopheles mosquito, its poisonous bite and its manner of breeding in stagnant pools, is regarded by them as mere tall talk. It is to lessen the chance of malaria that it is advisable to clear away as much bush as possible from around the villages.

Remedies for existing evils. The great need is for Government action, drastic, decisive and immediate. Nothing short of this will avail to save the Melanesians from extinction. Missionaries can do little or nothing to prevent it because they have no power to make or enforce laws dealing with purely secular matters. If the suggestions I make are regarded as Utopian and impossible, I venture all the same to make them because they seem to me the only ones that will effect what we want, viz. the salvation of the Melanesian race.

(a) In the first place we require a political settlement so that we may know where we stand. The Condominium Government is a compromise. But compromises and half measures are no longer possible. Fortunately the British and French Governments have now been so drawn together that there should no longer be room for international jealousies. But if the islands are given to the French which, I suppose, is a possibility, I fear we can do nothing unless some strong appeal is made, by people in high position, to the French Government to reform their rules and exercise sterner measures against those who transgress them.

(b) We need a responsible official of some sort attached to and resident in each group of islands or at least to a district not too large to be kept under close observation.

(c) Recruiting should be properly regulated and at times prohibited, especially in the Torres Islands. There should be proper inspection of all plantations and enquiry into hours of work, repatriation of time expired labourers, etc.

(d) Sumptuary laws should be enacted. As has already been mentioned, sumptuary laws of a harmful kind have been made. These enforce the wearing of clothes. We need sumptuary laws which restrict the use of European clothes. Such goods as trousers, shirts and coats should be forbidden, or so heavily taxed as to make the price prohibitive to ordinary natives. The Fijian *lavalava* might be encouraged.

(e) The sale of all intoxicating liquors should be forbidden and offenders against this rule severely punished.

(f) Government hospitals should be erected and means afforded of getting to them.

(g) Government stores should be set up where tools, soap, and drugs such as quinine, can be bought by the people at reasonable prices.

(h) The natives should be stimulated to help themselves to develop waste land and not submit tamely to remain as servants to planters or give up their land to European speculators. Encouragement in this way would lead to the clearing of land round villages. The people might come to see the value of co-operation and so the universal distrust which now prevails might break down. The feeling that government officials are friends, and not merely policemen, would go far to giving a stimulus to enterprise.

(*i*) Some kind of bonus might be given to people of energy and to parents of large families.

I have no doubt that some of these recommendations will be thought absurd. But I contend that if we undertake to rule any people at all, we must act towards them, especially when they are helpless as these people are, in a tender and fatherly way. We have no right to assume the position of governors otherwise. We need more than the negative and repressive rule which now prevails here. The Resident Commissioners are more of the nature of glorified policemen than rulers. Their actions seem mainly confined to punitive measures and expeditions. Natives die by the thousand as the result of the white man's acts and nothing is done. One white man dies by the hands of some lawless natives and instantly the authorities are awake, the native police are marched out, men-o'-war steam up, and the misguided natives are hunted to death, their gardens trampled down, their pigs shot, their villages desolated. Of positive help towards a better life these people receive nothing.

As a Church we are apathetic, but we seem helpless in face of the difficulties. We need to arouse in the hearts of all humane people a conscience towards a child race such as this is. Our efforts to help them are at present wholly inadequate and we ought not to be content merely with trying to alleviate the miseries of their latter end. As Bishop Gore has recently said: "The Church has constantly been occupied in picking up the wounded in the battle of life—in providing medicines and staunching wounds—when it ought to have been thundering at the gates of tyranny" (*Religion of the Church*).

Apart from all considerations of humanity, it is to the advantage of the Government to save the native race. These islands without a population are entirely useless. No indentured labour from outside is likely to be obtainable. Recent legislation with regard to Indian coolie labour in Fiji has put the extinguisher on any trader's dream of getting such labour here. If Japanese and Chinese come (and some have found their way already to these islands) they will not come simply to help the white man to get rich but will come as masters in their own right. If they will fulfil towards these children of Melanesia an elder brother's part which we are too supine and indifferent to undertake, then the sooner they come the better.

III

DECADENCE AND PRESERVATION IN THE NEW HEBRIDES

By Dr Felix Speiser

THE fact that the natives of the New Hebrides are rapidly decreasing in number cannot be disputed. This is to be regretted both from a humanitarian and a commercial standpoint. The greatest efforts should be made to preserve the remnant of the people; and this more especially, as the advent of the white man has undoubtedly contributed to the decrease. Internal decadence may have set in before the settlement of the white man in the group, for the native customs and practices must always have tended towards this; but on the other hand, it is certain that an impetus was given to it by the arrival of the white, one or two generations ago. It is therefore necessary to look for a causal connection between the two facts—to consider the agencies of extermination, and discuss their relation to the settlement of the white.

The islands especially to be considered are the Northern New Hebrides and the Banks Islands; and in weighing the value of my observations it must be remembered that there are no trustworthy statistics. They must be accepted as the personal views and impressions of one who has the natives' welfare at heart, and who has spent two years enquiring into the conditions of life in the group. The writer trusts that most of his conclusions will be accepted by impartial observers, and may prove of use to those who have the right to legislate for the people.

The subject may be discussed under the following heads:
Decrease caused by:

1. Disease.
2. Harmful development of native customs.
3. Indirect influence of the white.
4. Direct influence of the white.
5. Improved conditions necessary.
6. Definite propositions.
7. Objections anticipated.

Disease. This subject could only be adequately dealt with by a medical man, but as this has never been done, the views of a layman must be taken for what they are worth; and this is permissible as the diseases are treated in a very general way. Alcohol is included under this heading, as its action on the native is that of a disease.

Diseases of the respiratory organs may first be considered, as they are undoubtedly claiming the most victims, chiefly in the form of tuberculosis, influenza, bronchitis and pneumonia. They are carried by ships from anchorage to anchorage and from island to island, and a slight cough or cold, hardly noticed on the vessel, may and frequently does, develop into a very destructive epidemic in islands such as these which have little contact with civilisation. Certain isolated islands are periodically swept by dangerous epidemics of bronchitis and influenza, upon the arrival of ships; and the number of deaths is often very great. For this cause we may assume a decrease in the population before a white settlement has actually been made, and before the people have become acquainted with European remedies. In Santa Cruz, for instance, where only one white man is at present settled, the population is fast diminishing through colds brought by visiting ships. It is estimated that in Graciosa Bay the population is only half what it was some seven years ago.

It seems that after some years the natives become less liable to infection, or that an increased traffic makes the outbreaks more endemic; though from time to time they again assume an epidemic nature, and quickly spread from the coast inland, and from island to island. Whole villages are attacked so that hardly a native is unaffected. Many succumb and a tendency to pneumonic troubles and consumption remains.

These diseases have certainly been imported by the white, and are probably responsible for half the deaths in the islands. Obviously, the restriction of these diseases would be a great step in the preservation of the natives. As they act on the aboriginal almost as violently as dysentery and measles, quarantine regulations would be quite justifiable though scarcely practicable. The only hope is that the remaining natives may become immune to these diseases, and may learn to resist them as white men do. Pneumonia and bronchitis are largely caused by the carelessness of the natives—when overheated, for instance, or after a wetting. They drink from the same bamboo, exchange pipes and eating utensils, and thus promote the spread of coughs and colds.

Dysentery, small-pox and measles are now happily rare, as compared with earlier years, when they ravaged the group terribly, and depopulated whole districts and even islands. They were certainly introduced by the white, and that they spread so alarmingly may be due to the causes mentioned under pulmonary diseases, and to the facts that they were introduced to virgin soil, so that the natives were unable to offer a good resistance and thus check the spread of the sickness. More recently, due probably to harbour-control, there has been much less sickness of this nature in the islands; and there is no reason why it should again increase if ordinary precautions be taken; so that this class of disease may be disregarded in considering the future welfare and preservation of the people.

Malaria is known on almost every island of the New Hebrides, though of course it is more prevalent in the lowlands of swampy districts. It does not appear that malaria does much harm directly, though doubtlessly it lowers the vitality of the natives and makes them less resistant to other infections, especially when the natives are transferred from one island to another.

It is very doubtful whether malaria was introduced by the white, and in any case it does incomparably more harm to them than to the natives, to whom it may be regarded as a small destructive agent. Black-water fever is not frequently met with, and is consequently of no importance to the race.

Leprosy and elephantiasis have been confined to certain districts, often villages, but are still very frequent and have sometimes caused many deaths. Still, these diseases are not very virulent; or, considering the innumerable means of transmission, they would have spread more alarmingly. As it is, they do not increase the death-rate in any perceptible degree.

Sterility is frequent, and has probably always been so, but tends to increase through various causes which have only recently become operative, which will be discussed later.

The death-rate of infants must always have been abnormally high, because of the injudicious feeding with yam and taro at an early age. But to this must now be added the considerable mortality through sickness, newly introduced, which is felt especially by the children.

Venereal diseases have without a doubt been introduced by the white man. It is difficult to estimate their prevalence in the group, as the natives are naturally reticent; but as might be expected they are found more frequently in some districts than in others.

Personally I have met with very few cases of syphilis, and am inclined to think that it is not common; though when remembering the opportunities and the kind of white man who has had intercourse with the natives, and the facilities for spreading infection, it is surprising that so many healthy natives are to be found in the group. It is well known how unscrupulously recruited women are used by some whites, and how they become more or less common property on certain plantations. It is known too that many boys return from plantations to their homes thoroughly diseased. What then prevents the spreading of the disease, and how are we to account for the comparatively healthy state of the natives? It seems that acute syphilis leads to a speedy end, and as there can be no propagation it destroys itself automatically. But in spite of this we must credit this class of disease with a great part of the destruction of the natives. The population of Aneityum, for instance, is said to have been to a great extent destroyed by syphilis.

There is no need to dwell on the evil effects of alcohol on the natives. It kills directly through poisoning and indirectly through sickness and quarrelling. It cannot be denied that whole districts, as for instance Ambrim and Omba, have been depopulated, and its baneful influence has been almost as great as tuberculosis. It is a source of surprise and regret that legislation has failed to suppress the consumption of alcohol in the islands, and that its sale still continues more or less openly. Undoubtedly a determined effort on the part of the British and French Governments would put a stop to this once and for all. It is true that many settlers refrain from selling alcohol, but by no means all do what is in their power to suppress the traffic on the part of their neighbours. The only men who have never tired of fighting the sale of alcohol are the missionaries, for which they deserve the thanks of every well thinking man.

Unhappily some of the missionaries go to the other extreme, and consider kava as harmful as alcohol. Kava is drunk very moderately in the New Hebrides, and to judge from the effects on the natives of the more westerly islands, it does very little harm, except when taken in excessive quantities. There are not a few kava drunkards in the islands, but these are usually old men, with few other joys in life; the rest of the people occasionally gather for kava-drinking bouts. Some of them may become drunk (though this does not mean that its effects are as injurious as those of alcohol), but they will afterwards keep sober for weeks. Also the local method of preparation does not permit a man to drink excessively, and in old times kava-drinking was restricted to natives of high rank and to periods of special festivity, and it is still forbidden to women.

It is therefore not right to attribute to kava a share in the diminution of the people; and it is a question whether its use in moderation might not be permitted in order to allay the craving for alcohol.

European food and clothes add indirectly to the death-roll as agents in the spread of disease. It may be observed that wherever the natives have given up the old vegetable diet, and are living mostly on rice and meat, their health is not good. A too-strong meat diet causes boils and other complaints, and the cessation from garden-work deprives the people of wholesome occupation and encourages idleness with its attendant evils. It would be good if the sale of European foods could be forbidden except in times of famine.

Without statistics it is impossible to prove that clothing is harmful, but according to our modern views of hygiene, dirty clothing is an agent in the spread of disease. Very few natives realise the danger of spending the day in wet clothes, and rarely change them when wet. Women frequently wear several dresses, which are often soaked on rainy days. The people usually work and sleep in the same suit of clothes. This must be injurious to health, and yet some deny it. The danger is not very obvious because in the native environment there are so many agents for the transmission of disease. Where, however, the situation is so precarious, the smallest detail is of importance, and the wearing of clothes should be discouraged. Traders find a profit in the sale of clothing, and encourage its use; and missionaries (except to some extent those of the Anglican Church) do not disapprove; some even go so far as to make clothing a condition of baptism.

It cannot be too strongly urged upon the missionaries and traders that clothing is unnecessary for the natives in their natural environment. Everything should be done to keep the people natural and unaffected, and to prevent a false modesty and artificiality. It cannot be said that modesty is encouraged by the wearing of clothes; perhaps even the reverse is true. Those who encourage the use of clothing should bear in mind that so long as its absolute harmlessness has not been definitely proved, they may be under the awful responsibility of accelerating the death of these people, whose preservation should be their primary aim. The people do not possess an unlimited supply of clothes to take the place of wet, torn and dirty garments, and they have not the means of mending and cleaning foul clothes. One of the most pathetic contrasts in the islands is the lithe and glossy skin of the healthy native and the dirty, over-dressed Melanesian masquerading as a white man.

The following is probably the order in which the destructive agents already considered should be placed, according to their injurious effects on the natives: disease of the respiratory organs; dysentery, small-pox, measles (in the past); alcohol; venereal disease; infant mortality; European clothing and food.

Harmful development of native customs. In addition to considering the diseases, and especially those introduced by the white man, we must study the native customs and determine what proportion of blame must be apportioned to them, *i.e.* how far the race would have destroyed itself if it had been left alone. There is a noticeable decadence in the culture of the people—a decadence which may date back long before the arrival of the white settler—and this suggests the possibility that the decay was not restricted to the social, but also had its effect on the physical domain.

The killing of widows has been an important agency. Only the widows of chiefs were killed in the northern part of the group, in Santo and the neighbouring islands. In the south the custom was practised in Aneityum, and spread to Tanna, Eromanga, etc. Much harm has resulted from the fact that latterly not only the chiefs' wives were killed, but all widows. It is evident that this custom, by embracing all ranks, jeopardised the race before the arrival of the first missionaries; as it led to a great scarcity of women. For example, on Aneityum the proportion was said to be six females to ten males. But it is equally evident that the custom cannot be old, or the population would never have increased. The custom occurs in Santo in an early stage, and it cannot have done much harm there. It is to be remembered that in earlier days chiefs were not as numerous as they now are; and that the women killed after a chief's death formed but a small percentage of the total female population.

The present appalling shortage of women is due largely to

other causes, though it cannot be denied that had the practice spread, as it did in Aneityum, the consequences would have been similarly disastrous; but fortunately in other islands the widows of chiefs only, and not of commoners, were killed.

The natives have probably always known how to procure abortion, but its practice was always severely condemned, as it still is in uncivilised parts of the islands. During the last generation or two there has been a marked increase, which is certainly not a normal development of the old practice, but is connected in some way with the settling of the white in the group. This will be dealt with later.

In old days abortion was induced by women living in polygamic conditions, in order that they might escape the pain of labour and that the care of children might not be added to their many duties; occasionally as an act of revenge on a brutal husband. But the practice was not common, and there are certain proofs of a high birth-rate in earlier days.

Sterility was due partly to the long suckling of the children, partly to the hard manual work of the mothers; but the dense population of a few generations ago proves conclusively that abortion and sterility did no more than check the overcrowding of the islands. Infanticide was not common, and was the result of over-work, and of the contempt felt for twins, females and late-born children.

But these must all be considered as irregularities; nothing suggests the possibility that they would have become dangerously frequent customs, had not the social and domestic ties of the people been interfered with.

The low birth-rate is due in part to the scarcity of women, and in part to the fact that in each village a few old men may have all the women. It is due in part too, to the fact that the girls become mothers at a very early age and are prematurely sterile; in part it is due to the polyandric conditions and general licence. Until a few generations ago, however, the people increased in numbers, and the islands carried a strong, healthy population; so that these agents cannot have had the ill-effects on the population which they obviously have at the present time.

In earlier days sexual intercourse was almost always very strictly regulated; much more so than is now the case. The man had a moral right to commit adultery if he was prepared to bear the consequences; but, generally speaking, the customs and laws of the village made illicit intercourse a matter of extreme difficulty. The men always lived together, and the absence of one of their number would immediately excite suspicion, as would his presence in the women's quarters. Many eyes would be interested in his movements, and if he was detected, he would almost certainly be killed by the husband. The morals of the people are now loose. But this was not the case in former times, when the natives lived naturally; the old customs were adhered to, and penalties were exacted for infringing the laws governing their domestic relationships. Though their system of morality was different from that of the whites, it was undoubtedly a check on licence. It is the attempt to force our views on them by precept and example, intentionally or unintentionally, which has broken down their old system; for where white influence has been most felt, and the old law of revenge has been abolished, the morals of the people are slackest. It is a fact that in some places sexual intercourse was forbidden, even between husband and wife, at certain stated intervals; though of course there were periods of the year when there was general freedom, and the wives of polygamists became the common property of the young men of the village.

Prostitution was only practised openly in a few islands, and though the public harlot was not unknown, there has been an increase in this direction through contact with the whites. When money passed, this was always in secret. But more generally prostitution assumed rather the form of hospitality, and guests were openly and as a rule freely provided with women by their hosts who, being in a position to make feasts, usually had the majority of the women. So it has followed that the shortage of women among the ordinary men through polygamy and other causes, led to polyandric conditions—for polygamists lent their women as rewards for services rendered, and to retain the goodwill of the young men. It is a fact that the present laxity is the direct outcome of contact with the white man, and is the consequence, not the cause, of the decadence of the people. One of the evil results of the shortage of women, especially on some plantations, is the prevalence of unnatural offences—and this is a call to those in authority to require and provide conditions which shall, as far as possible, eliminate temptation from the lives of men and boys employed as labour on the plantation.

It has been confidently affirmed that the diminution of the people is due to too close inbreeding. As a matter of fact there is an exogamic system which prevents close inter-marriage and connection between relatives within certain degrees of consanguinity. This system is rigorously followed. It is very rarely indeed that the bounds are crossed, and when they are, the irregularity is recognised and the offenders are treated as outcasts—in that they have excommunicated themselves from the social economy of the community. Throughout the group there is no confusion, as each individual knows his particular position in the system and his relation to all other natives. Visitors and settlers from other islands take the same status as in their own homes without hesitation or question. This system is so nearly perfect, and has been in vogue for so many hundreds of years, that it may be omitted from this consideration of the agents of destruction of the people.

Some think that fighting is responsible for the decimation of the natives. This is true—but chiefly since the introduction of firearms. Fighting has continued for centuries, and yet on our arrival in the islands we found a dense population, where now whole tribes have disappeared, and large districts have become depopulated. In old days the wars were not very serious; the skill of the aggressor was usually equalled by the defender's skill in dodging his arrows and spears; and as a rule fighting ceased when each side had lost five men. Fighting in ambush (the usual native method) was as dangerous to the attacker as to the attacked, so long as native weapons were used—but with the rifle an advantage was given to one party and the terrible war of extermination began, which has reduced the people in some parts to a tithe of their former strength. Killing became a regular sport.

The same may be said of murder. There have always been quarrels, and these from time immemorial have ended in bloodshed. It cannot be said that new and more effective poisons and other means of committing murder have been introduced; but new subjects for quarrel have arisen, and the consequence is that since the white man's arrival, murders have become more common in some parts of the New Hebrides. This will be considered again later, but for the present it is sufficient to bear in mind the fact that internecine warfare and secret murder could not possibly have depopulated these islands if ordinary native weapons had continued to be used, as was the case when the people flourished and the population was dense.

It seems that no one of these so-called destructive agents

can truly be said to have had a real part in the present sad condition of the people. If their marriage, social, and domestic systems had not been interfered with, they would have continued to increase and multiply as in former years. So it must be frankly owned that the native is not responsible for his own disappearance, and we must go on to consider the effect of extraneous circumstances, and especially the influence of the white immigrant on the people of these islands.

Indirect influence of the white. This influence manifests itself principally in the loosening of the social ties which formerly kept the people under restraint. There has never been a definite prohibition of many of the old customs and habits of the natives, but contact with the white man has led to a steady depreciation of the social organisations of the people, together with a pitiable attempt to ape the white man. A native race soon becomes aware of the weakness of its civilisation, and naturally becomes the more dissatisfied the longer the superior race refuses to incorporate the inferior into its own system. In the New Hebrides we have an extreme example of tardiness in incorporating the weaker race, and a consequent disturbance of former conditions with a lack of efficient substitutes to preserve order. We can imagine an ideal contact between a low and a high standing race, where the former would not receive injurious elements from the latter (as for example disease and fire-arms); but we cannot picture an intercourse where the lower people would not be forced to compare their own organisations with those of the superior people, with the consequent contempt for their own. This subtle influence of the whites on the social condition of the natives must be followed out carefully. The chiefs were both respected and feared by the people—respected because of their supposed supernatural powers. The white man scarcely discriminated between the chief and his people, and certainly never respected him, or feared his knowledge of the unseen. He protected himself with his superior weapons, and had the moral support of his man-o'-war behind him. He proved himself the stronger, without having to resort to magic and witchcraft. The chief's power was undermined, and faith in the supernatural was broken down. In a civilisation built on belief in the unseen, and ordered by the power of the chief, the white man's advent was followed by the gravest consequences. Secret ceremonies of the utmost importance to the natives were laughed at by the white; old customs were treated with scant respect; and social institutions (*e.g.* the Suqe and Qat—native "clubs") were degraded by the rudeness and ignorance of the white, and by his discouragement of native etiquette among his own boys. Thus the white man usurped the place of the chief and disparaged the social economy of the natives.

Again, the white man could not be touched by the native charms; he entered with impunity the most holy places; he was present at the most awful ceremonies, and handled the most sacred objects, which hitherto only natives of the highest ranks had been allowed to see—and he always came out unscathed. He proved himself superior to the religious system of the people on every occasion. As a necessary consequence, faith in their ghosts and spirits was weakened, and sceptics began to ask if there really was anything in their system after all.

Later, natives returned home from centres of white civilisation, where they had been impressed by the superiority of the white man and the comparative magnitude of his works. They had adapted themselves to the white man's mode of life, and on return to their homes were sadly impressed with the comparative emptiness of their own civilisation. They could not continue to respect the chief and fear his power. Imagining themselves somewhat superior to those who had stayed at home, they endeavoured to take the place of the chief, and succeeded in still further undermining his power—in a word they became anarchists. The valuable tusked pigs, the means by which higher rank could be obtained might now be procured by young men with the money they had earned on plantations in Queensland and Fiji; and positions, formerly filled by old men after a life of shrewdness and intrigue, might now be filled by young men, possessing none of the secrets of that strength which had made the earlier chiefs a real power, and worthy of respect.

Every third man became a sort of chief; and the old "caste" system which hitherto had resulted in men of strong personality and character filling the office of chief was swept away without a thought. Old sacred practices—cannibalism, vendetta, widow-killing, etc.—were forbidden by missionaries and others, much to the disgust and chagrin of the old chiefs. They found, on the other hand, that all the old restraints and checks on licence and immorality had gone, and that there was a dissolution of all that had kept the people together and prevented excess. On the other hand, they found their own power was undermined and that they were quite unable to cope with the changes in the old order. They may have put forth their best efforts to arrest the downfall of the native institutions, but opposition daily became stronger and they themselves less able to offer resistance. Patriotism and loyalty were now things of the past, and all the cords which had united the people into a community and a tribe under a recognised head were snapped; and it became easy for each man to follow his own inclinations, without thought of the public good and the honour of the tribe.

It cannot be pretended that the chiefs were perfect. They were often tyrants of the first order; but they certainly preserved discipline and put down insubordination. They controlled the affairs of their districts, and in a modest way administered justice; as far as possible they eliminated disturbing elements which tended to diminish the fighting power of the tribe. With their downfall, young hot-headed youths came into power; and instead of aiming at the preservation of the tribe, each strove for the place of the ousted chief, with a natural increase in lawlessness, feuds and murder—which increase was unfortunately enhanced by the simultaneous introduction of fire-arms. Whilst formerly war was discussed by the assembly of the men, and the strength of the tribe was carefully estimated, now the individual did not hesitate to involve the whole village in his own affairs and make it responsible for his misdeeds. The villagers had perforce to take sides, family ties were broken, and the people began to split off into the small hamlets one sees to-day. These small bodies of natives are demoralised and dejected. They have none of the tribal traditions and old associations left. They are convinced that their days are numbered; that they have no future as a race; that they are neither wanted nor needed. What wonder is it that, discouraged and dispirited, the women refuse the cares of motherhood, and the men do nothing to preserve the old traditions and customs, to keep the sacred buildings in repair and provide for future generations? Is it fair to draw attention to the increase of lawlessness, where the people have no law—to the increase in immorality and infanticide, where there is nothing to deter them, and so little to encourage them to live for the future? Is it necessary to pursue the question further, or is it granted that the white man has had some share in the deterioration of this people and the depopulation of the islands?

If this is granted, it must be owned that we must do something to counteract the prevailing anarchy. It remains as the first duty of those who have helped to bring about this most deplorable state of affairs—be they government officials, missionaries, or planters—to make every attempt to restore to the people the comparative liberty and security of earlier days by re-establishing the old authority of the chief; or if this is impossible (as it probably is) by giving them as a sufficient substitute the law of the white man in its entirety, based on a sensible appreciation of native requirements. Besides this, something must be given them to fill the vacancy in their lives we have caused by ridiculing the objects on which their faith was centred. Instruction on a religious basis seems the best way of providing them with an ideal to aspire to. With this and a restoration of law, the people will be given an object in life, and a reason for preserving their old traditions and customs for future generations.

Direct influence of the white. There are five classes of white men who directly influence the natives—recruiters, traders, planters, missionaries, and government officials, and it remains for us to consider the influence they respectively exert on the people.

It is unnecessary to recall how recruiting was carried on in early days; or to dwell on present-day recruiting; as to how far the laws which are supposed to regulate it are respected. It is proposed rather to examine the effects of recruiting on the people as it is carried out to-day under "Condominium control."

The native engages himself to work (generally for three

years) to a certain master for a certain wage; and the employer promises to provide food, lodging, medicines, and—it is understood—safety.

The motives for going to work on plantations given by the natives are: (1) curiosity to see the world and to enjoy the supposed freedom of plantation life; (2) desire for money; (3) to escape persecution and punishment for lawlessness. These motives are not bad in a wild country or in a new colony, where by engaging as labour the people can travel and see something of the world. But the system has very unsettling effects in a newly pacified group like the New Hebrides.

The opportunity to travel has long since lost its attraction, for the native can satisfy his globe-trotting instincts by sailing in safety from island to island in his own boat. It is very seldom indeed that a native is so simple as to be coaxed by a recruiter to share in the "jolly" life on a plantation.

The need of money is not felt except in a few districts where coconuts are scarce, and the people can make considerably more from the sale of copra than on the plantations, and the natural inclination is surely to get the most they can in the easiest way.

There remains then the third as the principal reason for recruiting, *i.e.* the evasion of persecution and punishment, or to put it in other words, the present system is based on entirely wrong principles, for it protects outlaws on the one hand, and encourages lawlessness on the other. Many boys are not happy in their own homes, because for some reason they do not fit into the village life. Others are not safe because they are continuously running foul of native laws and customs. Often a boy recruits with a woman, perhaps because of some quarrel of hers with her husband, perhaps because he has wronged her. For various causes large numbers of natives desire to leave their homes for a time, and the recruiting vessels give them the opportunity they need to disappear till time has healed their differences.

On the one hand, we have the Government administering law and the missions striving to pacify the islands, and on the other, a body of men who benefit by every unlawful act and every trouble and disorder in the native life. It is no wonder that these two parties are opposed to each other, and that the progress of civilisation is so tardy. The missions are often accused of acting against the recruiters, but it is patent that if the islands are to be pacified, the natives must be kept at home. The quieter the islands, the less chance have recruiters to obtain labour, but it is scarcely fair to blame the missionaries for withholding their boys from the plantations. That disorder is the best friend of the recruiter is shown by the fact that the vessels collect where there is least civilisation and where there is discord and strife. If there is peace and order they must perforce create trouble— *e.g.* they must distribute alcohol and fire-arms, and be on the spot to collect the fugitives from native justice. As an outcome of this, there is bad feeling towards the whites as a whole; for the elder natives have a grievance in that the boys and girls have left without their permission.

Then again, the term of engagement is too long. Few natives realise what they do when they sign for three years, for the native does not think in years. They become estranged from their homes. Their relatives die, and perhaps their village may disappear. They forget their old mode of life and become attached to the "freer" life of the plantation. Their gardens become overgrown; their houses fall into decay; their possessions fall into other hands; they are forgotten. If they return at all, they find themselves with a certain sum of money and a miscellaneous collection of gaudy articles, but homeless and friendless. Having no gardens they are dependent on the hospitality of others, and soon realise that they are a burden and not wanted. The consequence is that they again recruit on the first vessel that puts in an appearance. They may be extremely useful for the upkeep of the plantations where they are employed, but as far as the upkeep of the native race is concerned they are absolutely useless.

Another point is to be remembered. When escape from punishment is made so easy, is it not a strong encouragement to lawlessness in the islands? The recruiting vessel is a city of refuge for the offender, and this he knows before he commits a crime; and the question may be asked, does he not sometimes commit a crime *because* he knows it?

The question of the mortality of recruits should be treated under the head of plantations, but it must be stated that the proportion of natives who return to their homes at the expiration of their term of service is very small, although there are unfortunately no statistics to prove the statement. One French plantation is said to have a mortality of 40 per cent. per annum, and another to return only 10 per cent. of the number recruited. It is impossible to pretend that such a large proportion would have died in their own homes.

The natives who are recruited are lost for production of children, and generally they are the flower of the people. The islands cannot stand this continual drainage. Villages are known where all the youths have gone, and only the aged and the children are left to keep the village in good order. In S. Omba very many young women have gone to the plantations, and have only returned when too old for child-bearing. The lee sides of most islands are the more sparsely populated, because recruiting ships invariably anchor there; and places which were once the best recruiting areas are now nearly depopulated. Only districts not regularly visited by recruiters still carry a good population.

It is frankly acknowledged that much of the sad picture thus drawn is the outcome of the old "black-birding" methods of recruiting, and that now, as a rule, recruiting is much better regulated, and the "labour" receives much more attention and kindness than in former days; but those who desire the preservation of the natives cannot hope that a system which has so many "possibilities" for unscrupulous men and is based on unsound principles can long be allowed to interfere with the natural development of the islands.

Trading frequently goes together with planting, but their effect may be treated separately.

Copra-trading[1] is good in that it induces the natives to work, but it has its bad side in that the trader pays in kind; or—what amounts to the same thing—prefers to pay in kind; and creates as much as possible false needs, e.g. calico, kerosene, ironmongery, clothing and food. If the native could be forced to retain his old way of living, there would be a guarantee that he would be compelled to work in his own garden and grow his own food. Now he has only to make a little copra and change it at the trader's for rice and tinned meat.

Competition between the traders is so keen that the price given for copra has risen greatly; and this has had a bad effect on the people, in that they earn money much too easily, and consequently do not value it as they should. They spend it freely on any fancy which strikes them and have no idea of thrift and economy. They never accumulate sufficient to procure tools, implements, or stock. If money was not so easily earned, it would not be spent so thoughtlessly. On the one hand, it would become necessary for the

[1] "Copra" is a staple product, simply prepared from the coconut.

native to work hard to supply his needs; and on the other, it would make life much easier for the new settler, who is largely dependent on his copra trade until his coconuts come into bearing. In the interest of natives and traders alike it would be well if the Government would fix a maximum price for copra, and a maximum price for labour.

The planter exerts greater influence than the trader, as he brings his personality to bear on the lives of the boys and girls in his employ. A well-meaning man with ordinary commonsense can exert a good influence on his "labour." They are well-fed, clothed and housed, and live a regular life in clean and healthy surroundings. The natives return at the expiration of say three years, much improved by their stay on the plantation. Some learn to bake, build, tend horses, etc., and other trades; and, better still, the wholesome lesson that they have a place to fill in the world. But the evil influence of the unprincipled planter cannot be estimated. The labourers are badly treated. They are over-worked and under-fed, and crowded together in insanitary huts. There is never any discipline or control, and on leaving they are defrauded of their wages, and frequently kept long after the expiration of the time they have agreed to serve.

They learn all the rudeness of speech and behaviour of the baser kind of white planter; and by observing and imitating his vicious life, lose all respect for the white man, and all faith in religious influences.

But these are irregularities. They are abuses which might be stopped by efficient Government control, so that plantation life might well become a most useful experience in the life of the people.

It is not the fault of the planter that the native so soon forgets what good he had derived from his stay on the plantation. He comes into contact with his old conditions, and as his civilisation has not gone deep, he soon reverts to his native mode of life. There must, however, be something of refinement left which might prove to be a foundation on which to build up a stronger, more intelligent race of people in years to come.

If anything is strongly criticised it is the work which is being done by the missionaries in these islands. A body which makes the material and spiritual welfare of the natives its chief aim and object, works on a basis which is strange to all economic interests, and must be prepared for adverse criticism. Missionaries work for the salvation of the natives, and in consequence must at times come into conflict with the white settler.

It is unnecessary to speak of all the missions and the many denominations at work in the group. It will suffice for the purpose of the argument of this paper to refer to the work and influence of the Presbyterian Mission, which is the strongest mission in the New Hebrides.

The success of the Mission on the spiritual lives of the natives has no place in the matter under consideration, but it will be convenient to mention some of the successes and failures of the Mission with regard to the material welfare of the race during the fifty or sixty years it has worked in the group.

The Mission alone perseveres in the attempt to put down the use of alcohol; and it is entirely due to missionary enterprise that, though not completely stopped, the sale has been prohibited by law. It is due to the Mission that the labour traffic has been regulated and is now under some control, and it is not the fault of the missionaries that the improvement came somewhat late, and is not entirely satisfactory. They and their native teachers have penetrated far inland where the threat of the man-o'-war has no restraining power;

and their determined effort to pacify the natives has made it possible for planters and settlers to live unharmed. They have built several hospitals where the Mission doctors and nurses work with great devotion and splendid success; and they have built many churches and school-houses, and taught many hundreds of natives to read and write. That the motives of the missionaries are good can never be doubted, and that their success has been great is an unquestioned fact; but it is true that the methods employed are not always wise, or based on a careful study of the requirements of the people. It must be admitted that the Mission has failed to preserve the people. On very few stations has a serious attempt been made, for generally the missionary has limited himself to purely spiritual assistance. Where the attempt has been made, it has become abortive through the subtle influence of the "world." Mission stations may be regarded as creations of the missionary, where their word is law; but on examination we must acknowledge that few of them are as clean and healthy as they might be, and that the mortality is scarcely less than in the bush, and the birth-rate is certainly no better than in the inland villages[1]. As has been shown, the tendency of the natives is to adopt the white man's mode of life, food and clothing, and this tendency has frequently been encouraged by the missionaries. The natives are urged to use clothes and European food, and the neglect of their own industries and gardens naturally follows. It would seem to be a plain duty for the missionary to right this tendency in order to preserve the native. The life of the native on the station should prepare him to be independent of the white, and he should be given regular occupation and fitted to help other natives to live a natural, simple life. He is not compelled to work on the

[1] For evidence to the contrary, see p. 104. (ED.)

mission station, though presumably work is a component part of Christianity. The irritation of the planter in need of labour is excusable, when he sees lazy men idling away their time on the Mission reserves. It would certainly be an advantage to all parties if the Mission could so alter its methods as to include the interest of the white settler, even at the risk of introducing the natives to new temptations.

The ideal of many missionaries is to isolate their people from the influence of the world and keep them from contamination in Utopian conditions of perfection. But surely this is an impossible ideal; surely it is impossible to separate the people from the world and its temptations; and has a morality without temptation any reality and depth?

And the Mission school villages (*i.e.* as distinct from the head stations) can scarcely lay claim to any moral superiority. Intrigue and quarrels are not unknown, and their prevalence depends for the most part on the character of the native teachers in charge, who, frequently enough, keep their own interests in view and let the village affairs go as they will, or bully the people and lord it over them. The native needs a firm hand to keep him in check, but it must be a hand controlled by commonsense and justice. Formerly death was the punishment for heinous crimes, but now excommunication is substituted, and excommunication is not death. In this respect the influence of the Mission is similar to that of the recruiters, as it keeps an offender out of the reach of native law. It is regrettable that this should be so, and that the native teachers should have control of secular as well as spiritual matters, for it gives too much power for one native to have. But in this the Mission cannot be blamed, especially as in the northern portion of the group there are no real chiefs to assist in the government of the villages. The power of the chief depends on his knowledge of witchcraft and magic, and this power falls with his conversion, so that the native teacher has complete control of the village, and may use or abuse his opportunities for bettering the condition of the people.

Undoubtedly, it is a mistake to concentrate on the seashore, for many family and home ties are thereby stopped, and the new village is simply a collection of individuals with little in common and with no tribal enthusiasm. The feeling of homelessness, of being guests, produces a restlessness and insecurity which become chronic, though the people do not ascribe them to the break with their old way of life.

It may be said in summing up, that despite its good work, the Mission has perhaps interfered too much with the integral life of the people, instead of confining its beneficence to the religious domain. This may have been essential in days gone by when there was no Government control, but now the time has come to surrender secular affairs to the secular powers.

The Government has so far had practically no influence on the lives of the people. The man-o'-war occasionally threatens offenders and so gives weight to the arguments of peace-makers, and also deters the natives from over-impudent murder of white settlers by removing those who are clumsy enough to be caught. But the influence of the Government does not carry any further inland than the report of its guns. Only in the matter of recruiting can it be said that the natives are protected, and this statement only applies to the British Government. The native is unknown to the Government except as a recruit or a malefactor. No interest is taken in the people as a people. No attempt is made to better the condition in which they live. No effort is made to break down the centres of lawlessness, which are a continual danger to the coast tribes. For nine-tenths of the people government does not exist.

Summary and exceptions. We have now named all the factors which have operated on the once flourishing population of the New Hebrides during the past few generations, and have found that new diseases have been introduced; that certain customs have developed deleteriously through the introduction of new causes for quarrel and new means of adjusting it; that the white man has had an indirect influence in sapping the native life of its essentials, and a direct influence in making the life of the people more complex and difficult. It has also been pointed out that these observations apply chiefly to the islands in the north of the group. In the south the people are different in many respects, and have different customs, so that some of the remarks are not applicable to them, and they do not apply *in toto* to certain of the northern islands. For instance, there are certain islands, which seem to have survived the first contact with civilisation, where the population is now increasing, as for instance, Tanna, Malo, Paama, Merelava, and probably Tongoa. These are pleasant exceptions, and by tracing the course of improvement on one of them some hints may be gathered for use in arresting the decay of others.

Tanna was once an overcrowded island. It was almost depopulated by wars and recruiting (chiefly to Noumea) in a single generation. The Presbyterian missionaries succeeded in pacifying and Christianising the greater part of the island, and in checking the deportation of natives. The chiefs worked with the missionaries; and here their tenure of office is not dependent on knowledge of magic and the performance of religious rites. The chief's authority is based on hereditary principles, so that he does not lose his office on conversion. When a chief was converted he added his influence as chief to that of the Mission, so that he retained his authority and power over the people but used it in the interest of the Mission. Anarchy did not follow, but corporate tribal action under the chief continued as of yore. The white settlers were well disposed to the Mission, and the missionaries were discreet and allowed the development of the people to proceed naturally. A hospital was established, roads were constructed and maintained by natives under discipline. Confidence was felt in the missionaries, their advice was followed, and changes in the native mode of life were made where necessary. Old, infected huts were replaced by dry and airy houses on suitable sites, and the natives were taught to live simply in the native way, and to wear the modest loin-cloth only, except on Sundays. The health of the people improved. They became interested in their villages and vied with each other in keeping their houses neat and clean. New hope was infused into them, the birth-rate increased, and now the people are sufficiently strong, both morally and physically, to live without a resident missionary. It is true that everything favoured the efforts of the missionaries, and that the chiefs were men of real power and the people of superior intelligence; but the fact remains that the island of Tanna has weathered its vicissitudes, and there should be found help for assisting other islanders to happier conditions.

This desirable improvement was brought about:

(*a*) by patiently convincing the people of the necessity for change, *i.e.* by making them assist in their own salvation;

(*b*) by providing medical treatment;

(*c*) by building new villages in the native style, *i.e.* as especially suited to the natives;

(*d*) by preserving the old manner of life, *e.g.* dress, food, work;

(e) by recognising the chief's authority;

(f) by reviving self-respect, hopefulness for the race, and a reason for strenuous effort in Christianity.

The following notes and suggestions are based chiefly on the above hints derived from a study of the process of recovery in Tanna.

Measures suggested. Obviously the first aim should be to increase the population of the islands.

The birth-rate should by some means be increased. Abortion should be punished, and production encouraged—if necessary by a system of bonuses. The women should be equally divided among the men, not so much with the idea of stopping polygamy as to insure equal mating. Too early marriage should be prohibited. Weak and diseased natives should be prevented from marrying healthy women. People suffering from venereal disease should be isolated. Half-castes should always be treated as full-blooded natives.

The present system of recruiting is entirely unsatisfactory and should immediately be abolished and labour procured by other means.

It is not possible to return to the old mode of life entirely, but changes should tend to simplify life and make it more natural.

In the first place there would be a return to the old vegetable diet with its wholesome outdoor work. This should be made compulsory except in time of famine.

All products of civilisation, except those which have become absolutely necessary to the natives, should be strictly barred, and the natives thereby compelled to make for themselves mats and clothing, weapons and furniture. They should be encouraged, too, to raise stock and improve their gardens. Thus they would become attached to their homes and live industrious lives; and faith in themselves and hope in the future of the race would soon revive.

Improvements in medical treatment should be undertaken by a doctor, and when necessary should be made efficient by law. The doctor should not try to force the natives; but, as on Tanna, appeal to their intelligence, act with patience, and let all sanitary improvements grow out of their own wishes. It would be worse than useless for the doctor to plant his ideas on the unchanged convictions of the people. Though he should have the support of the Government when necessary, as a rule his treatment would be that of a counsellor and patient adviser, rather than of a government official.

This would require an official of a legal turn of mind. It is most important that the natives should be under control. The best conditions were undoubtedly those under which they flourished until half a century ago, but it is impossible to restore the chief and give him back his power. It is difficult enough to find trustworthy teachers, and it would be still harder to find chiefs. But as contemplated changes must aim as nearly as possible at a return to the conditions of happier days, natives should be placed in charge of the different villages, not as chiefs of the people, but as deputies of the Government and responsible to appointed officials.

In considering the welfare of the natives, we must not be blind to the needs of the white settlers; something must be devised which will suit all parties interested.

The necessity of providing the people with medical treatment and encouraging the birth-rate affects only the natives themselves.

The *recruiter* would protest against the establishment of law and order, but as the present system of recruiting is essentially wrong, there should be no recruiters to protest.

The *trader* would suffer from the return to the old way of living. He would lose much of his trade, and some compensation should be made to him.

The *planter* needs only sufficient boys to do his work. If these are guaranteed to him, he should have no grievance.

The *missionary* would not be handicapped in his work by means which touch only the secular life of the people, though it would become necessary for him to confine himself more to the spiritual side of his work. Certain sacrifices would have to be made, but no doubt these would be made willingly for the sake of preserving the natives.

The *Government* would be obliged to take an active interest in the natives, but this is more than is expected from a colonial administration. The conditions at Vila, the capital, should extend to all the islands of the group. This would mean a considerable increase in the staff of officials, and an increase in the cost of administration; and some means should be found to make the natives contribute towards the expenses incurred.

It is most emphatically stated at the outset that the following sketch of an administration makes no claim to originality or to be the last word on the subject. The writer does not presume to think he has solved the problem of the Pacific, but makes the suggestions based on a careful study of the facts already presented to the reader, to show how necessary improvements might find their way into practice. When a better scheme is submitted the writer will retire with alacrity, the more so as he is sincere in his efforts to help the natives, and his one wish is to contribute his quota towards making their lives happier, and restoring to them the peace which they have lost.

These propositions will strike many readers as being directly opposed to the old practices and traditions of British colonisation. The war having done away with many an old prejudice and having proved that in special circumstances interference of the Government with private enterprise is imperative and not always harmful, these propositions may sound to-day less preposterous than would have been the case in 1912. The basis of the proposed system is a severe supervision of the natives by the white authorities, a compulsion of the natives to work, and an export duty to pay the expenses of the whole administration.

The islands should be divided into convenient districts, e.g. on a population basis—one large island, or several adjacent small islands to constitute a district. Each district should be controlled by a district commissioner with police and necessary means of transport and communication, and should have a resident doctor with a simple hospital. The district commissioner and the doctor should periodically visit the whole district and take measures to improve the order and health of the people.

The doctor should be assisted by the district commissioner and should make a census of the natives and whites in his district, and keep a running register of births, deaths, and able-bodied natives in his jurisdiction. He should be assisted by native deputies or police, two in each village or sub-district, one being the recognised police agent, the other his assistant and to act as a control on him. Reports should be made to the district commissioner, but the police should have no executive power except in great emergency, e.g. bloodshed.

The police should receive a fixed salary, and should be responsible for the good order of their villages or sub-districts.

Marriages should be subject to the consent of the district commissioner with the doctor's approval, after the health and ages of contracting parties have been considered. Polygamy should be discouraged where women are in the minority. Women should not be allowed to marry at a distance from their homes. Offences against natural reproduction should be dealt with by the district commissioner, acting with the doctor's advice. Gratuities should be made to parents of large families, and advice given by the doctor with regard to the care of children.

The district commissioner should act as a Justice of the Peace; all cases should be adjudicated at headquarters, where the interests of the natives should be protected by a white advocate free of charge. The natives should be led gently and with as little compulsion as possible to understand the advantages of the new system. As little violence as possible should be used in order to secure the goodwill and interest of the natives. They should be shown that they are the inferior race, but should always receive justice, protection and humane treatment, and the whites should receive prompt assistance from the Government when necessary.

Trading should be under Government control in so far as the sale of articles not absolutely necessary to the natives is concerned. The maximum price for copra and other exports should be fixed by law and should not be exceeded by the trader, e.g. that of copra may be £8 per ton.

No white man should engage labour himself and personally, excepting in his own district, and then not for longer than four weeks (or two weeks when under conscription), without the sanction of the district commissioner. He should not be allowed to engage labour at all outside his district.

Recruiting should be entirely prohibited. Government should supply labour on demand of the settler at a fixed rate per month, and should be responsible for the good behaviour of the labourers and for their medical treatment. The employer should not be allowed to punish excepting in emergency, and should submit a report of the circumstance to the district commissioner.

Government should compel every able-bodied native over sixteen years of age to work during six months per annum, for a term depending on the demand for labour—say five years. Six months is suggested so that the native may not become alienated from his home and friends, and may give his garden necessary attention, especially as the sale of European foods is prohibited. During these five years the native should be considered as under conscription, and will be actually working for two-and-a-half years. As far as possible labour should be returned to their first employers, so that plantation work shall not be disorganised more than necessary. Labour should serve as near their homes as convenient so as to facilitate their return, and to enable them to visit their villages on one Saturday per month, which should be a full holiday from work. In this way they will keep in touch with their people, and married natives will be able to visit their wives.

Boys under conscription should be allowed to marry and their wives to accompany them to the plantations, the employers providing suitable accommodation, but the man must support his wife or wife and family unless the wife is employed at a fixed wage on work which does not interfere with child-bearing.

Girls who so desire should be placed with white women and employed in house work or slight garden work until they are sixteen years of age, when they should marry.

Men with more than three children should be free from conscription.

Natives, at the expiration of their term of conscription,

should be allowed to enter into engagements for terms not exceeding one year, and their wages increased with the permission of the district commissioner.

After the age of thirty-five years, the Government should have no further control over the native with regard to work and wages.

Natives with special knowledge of trades, *e.g.* baking, carpentry, coaching and stockmen, overseers and gangers, might receive a special wage-rate per month, so as to encourage the learning of trades and skilled labour.

The native should pay no taxes directly for the increased cost of administration. Direct taxation, *i.e.* a poll tax, is manifestly unjust where influential men can readily derive means whereby others pay for them, especially where some islands have an abundance of coconuts while others are without. The native should therefore pay his taxes indirectly by labour and a low maximum price for copra. Any convenient means might be employed by Government to collect the tax. One simple way would be to impose an export duty on copra of native origin. The same of course applies to any other product which it might be thought well to tax. The natives would not be any worse off with less money and fewer useless European articles on which to spend it. The trader would make more money than he does at present, owing to the maximum price of copra being fixed, and the planter would have regular labour at low wages and be rid of the trouble and expense of collecting it.

The Government should take no part at present in the education of the people, though their education would prove of the greatest benefit to them and to the settlers. At present the crying need is to save the remnant of the people, and compulsory education must come later. In the meanwhile the Missions would have an open field to continue their good work.

Legislators and statesmen will raise many real objections to the scheme outlined in this paper. Let its deficiencies be a challenge to them to compile something more practicable; it is the writer's sincere wish that it may be so. It will certainly be difficult at first to organise the system, but British colonisation has, I think, solved more difficult problems.

Objections of a more superficial nature will be urged against the scheme on the score of injustice. It will be asked whether it is just to give the natives so heavy a load, to compel them to work. Work is not degradation, and conscription is no more unjust than compulsory military service, *e.g.* in Australia and New Zealand. These islands have avowedly been acquired by the simple law of might. Theoretically we have no right to impose ourselves, our government and our moral code on the natives, who sold their land under a misapprehension, with no idea of forfeiting their autonomy and rights. If the fact of annexation is justifiable, it is equally just to administer these islands not only for our own benefit and advantage, but also for that of the native. The only truly just act possible is for us to withdraw from the group, and let the natives manage their own affairs. As this would involve the destruction of the people, the only alternative is for us to stay; to recognise that the people are our servants, and to treat them with humanity and kindness. The prosperity of tropical colonies demands that the native should do work which the white is unable to do for himself. If the settler did not need labour the problem would be simplified, but as he must have native workers it seems that compulsory labour is the fairest way to divide the burden amongst the people, and to make that burden as light as possible by treating them with consideration and respect. Besides being the fairest way of solving the problem, it is undoubtedly the kindest; for regular work is the one thing that the natives need to keep them robust and happy. Having disturbed their normal conditions of life, we must now act the part of the kind physician, and, as everyone knows, effective medicine has not always a sweet taste.

It may be thought by some that a simpler way out of the difficulty would be to introduce foreign labour, as was done in Fiji. But it would be as unnatural as it is absurd to carry labour for thousands of miles, when a sufficient supply is at hand and rusting for want of use. Moreover, few foreign peoples could work in the New Hebrides without suffering from the climate.

So the objection raised on the score of injustice should carry no weight, and the more so as irresponsible children are now permitted to bind themselves for a term of three years to serve a man they scarcely know. There is too much injustice in the present system to permit cant at lesser injustices in a proposed system of reform.

And lastly, in addition to the practical objections of statesmen, and imaginary objections of idealists, others who are usually apathetic and callous may be tempted to raise their voices against the changes proposed. These, withholding as they do their interest and sympathy, and incapable as they are of entering with enthusiasm into a scheme for the preservation of a charming people, should at least withhold their criticism, and not bring their opinions to bear against a scheme which though imperfect, may still be a finger pointing the way to something better.

IV

DEPOPULATION IN THE SOLOMON ISLANDS

By the Rev. A. I. Hopkins, Melanesian Mission

PERSONAL experience of some fourteen years in the Solomon Islands confirms the impression of a decreasing population. The decrease is not so great or so rapid, I believe, as that in the New Hebrides and Santa Cruz groups, but it is quite grave enough to justify alarm as to the future existence of the people. My own experience was gained on the island of Mala (or Malaita), the most populous and virile of the Solomon Islands, and the one on which the decrease is least obvious. But I fear that even there it is going on, and at an increasing rate. The causes are many and complex, and how to arrest the evil is a very difficult problem indeed.

To one living in Mala there are noticeable as main contributory causes:

A striking decrease in the size of families. Almost everywhere the previous generation seems to have been much more numerous, though the small islets off the coast still swarm with children. In inland villages they are very few in proportion to the much more scattered population. When trying to find causes for this there come to notice:

(*a*) *A growing postponement of marriage to a later age.* I suppose sixteen to eighteen was the normal marriage age some years ago; now marriage rarely takes place so early. The men wait till they have returned from plantation work, and then take a year or two to settle down. The girls are getting much more independent, and do not marry as ordered, but put it off. Probably on this account there is more immorality before marriage than previously.

(b) *Decrease in polygamy.* This tends to reduce the birth-rate, but I do not think it is at all a large factor in the matter. I do not gather that polygamy was very common or extensive in the old days. Probably in the New Hebrides it was practised on a larger scale.

(c) *Artificial restriction.* This seems to have been a known but rare and condemned practice in Mala before the coming of the white man. Now it seems to be spreading and to meet with less condemnation. The natives who have returned from Queensland have spread the practice, and added new methods of abortion to the old ones. Concoctions from the bark of trees are used.

(d) *Venereal disease.* Venereal sores are terribly common and syphilis must be playing a part in enfeebling and diminishing the population. But the evidence and observation of a doctor would be necessary to compute the gravity of this cause.

(e) *Dysentery.* This is a great scourge and a constant anxiety. More people probably die directly from this cause than from any other. Here I think there is hope of improvement, for our school villages escape more lightly than the heathen villages. Their people are more accessible and more amenable to advice, and can be taught, though of course very imperfectly, to use sanitary measures such as isolating patients, burning down huts, etc. The presence of a missionary is of great value here. Epidemics vary much in virulence; some sweep away villages wholesale; others pass, affecting only a few cases in the village. The percentage of deaths is also extremely variable. Santa Cruz has lately suffered terribly from this cause, and there has been very heavy mortality in San Cristoval also.

(*f*) *Pulmonary diseases*. It is very hard to judge whether these are more common, but probably it is so. The wearing of clothes, damp in heated huts, must aggravate these diseases, and the lessening vitality of the people tends to make resistance less effective. But statistically the death roll in Mala from this cause is not so very heavy, the people being more virile than those on the other islands.

(*g*) *Infant mortality*. Infanticide becomes less common, after birth at any rate, as Christianity spreads. But the death-rate of infants is very high. This is due mainly to sheer ignorance and foolish feeding. There seems hope of improvement here as the light spreads. On the other hand in places where food can be bought, infants are killed by being fed on tinned instead of natural milk, and rice instead of the chewed native food. There is a great opportunity for women's work here.

(*h*) *Plantation life*. This of course directly reduces the population by separating the sexes just at the marriage age. The girls are left behind, the men are congregated on plantations. Previously the exodus of men to Queensland had the same result. Now it is the gathering of males on plantations with a very small proportion of married men.

Behind all these overt causes of many deaths and a low birth-rate lies as the main cause the impact of civilisation on a primitive race, and its sudden contact with a far higher civilisation. Genuine Christianity alone can bring the two into harmony, raising the uncivilised and restraining the selfishness of the civilised. The old native life is losing vigour. Lessened fighting may have something to do with this, but the gain is far greater. It is the loss of interest in their own work, their own methods and their own lands. Life is made easier by money, wages, tools, etc., and there is temptation to idleness and slackness which the stress of existence corrected in the old days. The white man is the black man's burden; unless he uses great restraint, his presence saps the black man's independence. The Government as neutral between white and black can do much here to secure to the black man a fair chance. Work on plantations is no remedy; the natives simply endure an unnatural life for a time to get money. Very few are helped by it to a higher mode of life.

What can be done. Native marriage customs and morality should be respected both by Church and State. The old sanction of morality, fear of death, is going. New religious sanctions are only slowly taking its place. To encourage early marriage is most desirable. White men often misunderstand and therefore despise native customs that are helpful morally.

Sanitary action. This lies within the Government sphere, but missionaries can do much to help. Regulations as to pigs in villages, and as to general cleanliness help much to check dysentery.

Bringing greater interest into native life. If means could be devised by which the native worked more for himself and less for the white man it would be stimulating. If he could be encouraged by the formation of small native companies to make plantations of his own it would be a step forward. At present he only picks the coconuts that happen to grow, and sells them or makes a little copra. In Mala a good many of our new school villages have planted coconuts of their own, but not on any regular method. The selling of their land is very discouraging to native energy. The tenure of land is so complicated and uncertain that no one individual feels secure against sale. Nor do they readily grasp the meaning of absolute sale of land. It might be possible to set apart certain unalienable reserves, including some good coconut land, where the native would know he was secure and would find it pay to work for himself. Unfortunately the plantations require more labour than they can get, and the stay-at-home native is not in favour. It would be for the good of the natives if a far larger percentage of married people were on the plantations.

The Mission might do more to develop industry. When the new schools are established in the islands the teaching of carpentry with native timber might be developed; work in bamboo and garden work offer scope for teaching industry. Native industries might be encouraged. It might be possible in Mala to teach boat-building. The native now-a-days buys quite a large number of boats. If missionaries of the Mackay type could be found there would be a great work for them to do. By some such methods as these there seems a hope of averting the present rapid decrease. But the whole crux of the question is the relation of white to black. It can only be solved by more Christianity on both sides.

[67]

V

THE DEPOPULATION OF SANTA CRUZ
AND THE REEF ISLANDS

By the Rev. W. C. O'Ferrall

THERE is no doubt whatever that the population of this
district has decreased very greatly indeed since the days
when Bishop Patteson first visited it in 1856. The Bishop
refers frequently in his letters to "large crowds," "crowded
villages," "large crowds of men thronging the beach," etc.

My connection with these islands began in 1897 and it was
evident that a considerable change must have taken place.
Most of the Reef Islands were indeed still thickly populated,
so was the island of Trevannion. The large island of Santa
Cruz from Carlisle Bay on the north-east to C. Mendana
on the south was deserted. If one might believe native
accounts it had once been covered with villages. Graciosa
Bay and the south-west side were thickly populated and
from Graciosa Bay as far as Carlisle Bay there were a
number of small villages. About six years later, when I left
the district, a very marked decrease had taken place in the
big island of Santa Cruz, Trevannion, and in many of the
Reef Islands, notably Nukapu, Peleni, and Fenua Loa.

To what was this decrease attributable? The evidence of
older missionaries (like Dr Codrington) shows that the main
cause, previous to my sojourn, had been the labour traffic
and occasional epidemics. From 1897 the first of these may
be ruled out: these islands were placed under British protection in 1898 and very few Cruzians were recruited after
that date.

5—2

Pulmonary complaints were undoubtedly mainly responsible for the decrease. There were one or two bad epidemics of influenza, and one of dysentery which caused great mortality. One attack of influenza was, I remember, attributed by the natives to the visit of a trading steamer; it swept away large numbers of people about Carlisle Bay, several villages entirely disappearing.

The wearing of European clothes has been mentioned both in Mr Durrad's and Dr Speiser's papers as one of the factors which has contributed largely towards the depopulation. In my time very few of the Cruzians wore European clothes and therefore in these islands this custom, bad as it undoubtedly is, may be considered to have had a very limited effect.

Since 1904, when my connection with Santa Cruz came to an end, from all that one hears, the depopulation has increased rapidly. In a few of the Reef Islands where a vessel scarcely ever touches, the population seems to be maintained, but the Duff group is an exception, as through an epidemic—I think of influenza—there has been great mortality.

There is little doubt that unless something can be done, and done speedily, the native population will in another twenty years have almost died out.

VI

THE SOLOMON ISLANDS

By C. M. Woodford, late Resident Commissioner

IN the absence of any guide in the nature of a census return it is impossible to state with absolute certainty that the native population of the Solomon Islands has decreased during recent years, or is now decreasing, but my opinion, founded on what I remember of the number of natives living in particular localities thirty years ago compared with the number observed in 1914 is that there has been a considerable decrease, and in some cases there is no doubt of the fact.

I am of opinion that a decrease on certain islands, I refer to Ysabel, Russell Island and the west end of Guadalcanar, had been going on for at least three or four centuries, owing to the head-hunting and slave raids carried on in those islands by the natives of New Georgia and adjacent islands, and that from about the date of 1870 up to 1903 there must have been a decrease in the native population of the islands of Malaita, Guadalcanar, and San Cristoval owing to the emigration of natives to work on the plantations of Queensland and Fiji.

These two causes, having now ceased to operate, may be left out of the present consideration, but I think that in the whole of the Solomon group a decrease since the advent of the white man is in progress owing to changed conditions of native life, among which I give preference to the injudicious use of unsuitable clothing, which I am convinced is a fruitful cause of disease, and the introduction of new diseases, viz. dysentery, influenza and yaws.

The consequences of the contact of the native races with the white man have been serious to the native in other parts of the Pacific, as has been abundantly shown in the cases of the Hawaiian Islands, the Marquesas, Tahiti, Samoa, Tonga and Fiji.

The conditions under which the natives of Fiji lived previous to their intercourse with white men were very much the same as those obtaining among the natives of the Solomons. The population of Fiji was largely Melanesian, like that of the Solomon group, and it may therefore be presumed that similar causes would produce like effects in each case. It is therefore fortunate that a most valuable Report has been published entitled: *Report of the Commission appointed to enquire into the Decrease of the Native Population*, Govt. Printing Office, Suva, Fiji, 1896.

This *Report* should be in the hands of all attempting to deal with the causes contributing to the decrease of a native population living under like conditions, and it is fortunately accessible. It would appear from the *Report* above quoted that with a higher birth-rate than that of England and Wales the death-rate of infants under one year old was more than three times as high as the London death-rate, and that if the death-rate had not exceeded that prevailing in European countries there would have been an increase. In 1891 more than half the total deaths in Fiji were those of children. I believe that in the Solomons, while the birth-rate is high, a large number of the children die in infancy, and that the mortality among the whole population is excessive, owing largely to the diseases mentioned above.

Epidemic diseases. Measles, dysentery and whooping-cough have been the most fatal epidemic diseases in Fiji. Forty thousand died of measles in the great epidemic of 1875; whooping-cough in 1884 killed three thousand, and epidemic influenza and whooping-cough in 1891 accounted for fifteen hundred deaths.

Small-pox, so far as I know, has never occurred in the Western Pacific, in spite of a recent assertion that it has, nor, considering the rarity of its occurrence in Australasia and the rigorous measures taken for its suppression, is it likely to occur.

The Solomons have been happily spared such a fatal epidemic of measles as that referred to above. It was certainly brought to the group once by the Mission steamer 'Southern Cross' about the year 1898, but was confined, by quarantine, to the ship itself. On a later occasion a mild epidemic, supposed to have been measles, and with the characteristic rash, introduced from an unascertained source, caused great anxiety, in the total absence of any medical man. It affected almost all the natives employed in the Government station at Tulagi and spread elsewhere, but passed away without any ascertained fatal effects.

Dysentery of a most severe type is the most rapidly fatal disease in the Solomons. Death has been known to occur within three days of the attack. It is supposed in Fiji to have been an introduced disease. Whether that is the case in the Solomons it is impossible to say. One recent instance is known where it was certainly introduced from outside by a labour ship.

Influenza and the diseases resulting from it are responsible for many deaths in the Solomons and this disease is undoubtedly introduced afresh from time to time by ships.

The Polynesians even more than the Melanesians appear to be thoroughly aware that outbreaks of disease resembling influenza are likely to follow the visit of a strange ship. At the Polynesian island of Ongtong Java or Lord Howe's group near the Solomons, it used to be the custom as late as 1900 to asperge with ashes and water the persons landing from any ship to ward off the risk of disease, and I have myself submitted to the process on three or four occasions. Latterly the custom may have fallen into disuse as the group is more visited by ships than used to be the case.

Yaws (framboesia). Neither Mr Durrad nor Dr Speiser in their remarks refer to this horrible disease, but it assuredly occurs in the New Hebrides. It is probable that the visible effects of yaws are sometimes mistaken for those of another disease. In the Solomons it is common, although it is not believed to be of so universal occurrence as in Fiji where every child is infected with it sooner or later. The Fijian Commission attached such importance to this disease as a factor tending to the deterioration of the race that its conclusions may be quoted[1]:

(1) that yaws is a serious constitutional disease, the severity of which is lost sight of from the fact that it is almost universal among Fijians;

(2) that yaws and its sequelae are not only responsible for many infant deaths, but that they sap the vitality of the whole native race;

(3) that from its resemblance to syphilis we think it possible that it has an enervating effect on the child-bearing functions of native women;

(4) that, through familiarity with it, the natives have no fear of it as a disease of childhood; that they dread its appearance in adults; and that this has probably originated a universal belief that unless children acquire the disease they will grow up weakly and dull;

(5) that yaws occurring in the first year of childhood is almost invariably fatal;

(6) that the natives do nothing towards curing the disease,

[1] See page 163 of *Report.*

except when it is passing off, their idea of treatment being practically to allow it to saturate the system of its subjects;

(7) that the natives have no well-defined idea of its inoculability, but imagine it to be a disease that "grows out of the child." That almost all native children suffer from the disease for a period varying from three months to two years or longer; and that during that time no care is taken to cover or prevent the exposure of their sores, which thus serve as founts of infection;

(8) that the natives have no idea that the *sucuve*, *soki*, or *lovo* and *kakaca* (diseases which affect the feet) of adult life are the sequelae of yaws.

Dwellings. The native house of the Solomons is on the whole well suited to the climate if kept clean, and there are some excellent examples on Florida of what a native house ought to be; so the native can build a good house, and if he likes, can keep it clean. The floor of the ordinary Solomon house is the bare ground. The sleeping places are generally bedsteads raised on posts driven into the ground and raised from it about eighteen inches to two feet, which, however uncomfortable they may be, are better than sleeping on the ground itself. The ideal Florida house above referred to is raised on posts three feet or more above the ground and floored with an interlacing platform of split bamboo.

The water supply, unless it is drawn from a natural spring or running stream, is generally liable to contamination. It is in most cases an open well or waterhole entirely unprotected from the infiltration of filth and full of decaying vegetable refuse.

RECOMMENDATIONS.

It will be impossible for many years to come to make a census of the native population of the Solomons as a whole, but the Government should be asked to commence with the districts more directly under control and those under the influence of the resident missionaries of all denominations.

This would be no great task in such islands as Florida, Savo and others of the smaller islands, parts of New Georgia and the islands in the Bougainville Straits. Registers of births, marriages and deaths should be kept. Native ordained ministers should not perform marriages until their names had been registered for this purpose by the Government, in the same way that the names of white ministers are at present registered, and they should be responsible for furnishing the proper register of marriage to the Registrar. In the absence of civil officials, native or white, the registered native ministers might for the present also furnish the information required for birth and death records in their districts.

The Government should be invited to consider the expediency of taking measures to order the removal of houses and villages from insanitary situations and to order the closing of infected sources of water supply. In the case of villages situated in low land near the sea, the use of tube pumps might supersede the drawing of water from open wells and waterholes. As a rule in such situations there is an ample supply of water at a few feet from the surface. The cost of such pumps would not be serious and could be met partly by the natives themselves and partly by the aid of a Government subsidy. The sites for pumps should be selected by an officer versed in sanitary science and the work carried out by Government workmen. With the closing of contaminated sources of water supply it is believed that a diminution at any rate in the epidemics of dysentery would be brought about.

The medical advisers of the Colonial Office are fully alive to the seriousness of the disease of yaws in the Pacific and other tropical countries, and a new remedy for this disease, salvarsan, has recently been discovered. The results of experiment with the new formula have been encouraging.

Measures should be taken to prevent the misuse of unnecessary clothing. The use of heavy clothing of woollen cloth, such as is worn by white men in temperate climates and which the natives particularly favour, the fashion having been introduced by labourers returning from Queensland, might be rendered impossible by the imposition of a heavy customs duty on articles of this description. This would impose no hardship on any one, as the white man does not import such clothing for his own use, and the native could not purchase it if the cost were prohibitive.

The cotton waist-cloth, the *sarong* of the Malay, the Fijian *sulu* and the Samoan *lavalava*, is the proper garment for a native to wear, and in such a climate as the Solomons a man wants nothing else. The Wesleyan missionaries in New Georgia were encouraging the natives three or four years ago in wearing short trousers of calico. This was a step in the right direction, but the simple waist-cloth is preferable.

Natives living in contact with white men or under missionary influence think that a shirt or singlet is necessary. If these garments were ever washed their use would not be so much open to objection, but a Solomon Islander will wear them day and night, wet or dry, until they disintegrate into a network of holes or rags. They should be taught to do without body clothing. The missions have it in their own hands to discourage or even to prohibit the use of such clothing at school or in church. The sight of a healthy skin is more decent than that of a dirty shirt. The use of coconut oil for anointing the skin should be encouraged. It keeps the skin healthy, and prevents colds and parasitical disease such as ringworm.

In the case of a woman, a loose cotton blouse, hanging to the waist outside the waist-cloth, might be worn if it were considered necessary. This garment is known in Fiji as a pinafore.

If a native desired to be extravagant in dress he would have ample opportunity in a choice of waist-cloth of a quality superior to the ordinary trade calico at present imported for his use.

The advantage or otherwise of mosquito nets is doubtful. Certainly they are now required to be provided by regulation for natives working in the employment of white men on plantations. They have of course the advantage of protecting natives at night from the bites of mosquitoes, but the Fijian practice, where mosquitoes in the river deltas and coast districts are much more numerous than in the Solomons, of using a *sulu* as a coverlet for the whole body from the feet upwards when sleeping, appears to be preferable. Breathing over and over again the vitiated atmosphere confined within a screen measuring 6 ft. × 2 ft. × 3 ft. and enclosing about 30 cubic feet of air contained within a receptacle of dirty cheesecloth, the condition of which after a few days' use by a native can be easily imagined, cannot be healthy.

As warding off attacks of malarial fever, the mosquito net from a native's point of view may be left out of the question. It is probable that the blood of all natives in the Solomons is thoroughly impregnated with the malarial microbe from birth, and fresh infections by the bites of anopheles mosquitoes probably have little effect. It is not observed that natives suffer to any great degree from acute attacks of malarial fever. Among the white residents, on the other hand, it is very prevalent in an acute form, and frequently fatal.

Early marriages should be encouraged and married natives

accompanied by their wives and children might be permitted in some cases to engage as labourers on approved plantations where the manager was himself a married man whose wife would be willing to interest herself in the condition of the women and children. The women should not be allowed to do plantation work, but house work and laundry work in the manager's house of a light description would be of educational value.

The Government might be approached with the view of forming an industrial settlement in an approved locality under the control of a resident official. There are many homeless and masterless natives wandering about who loaf upon any village careless enough to entertain them. These men should be given the opportunity of making houses for themselves and wives should be found for them.

The heads of some of the large capitalist companies at present at work in the Solomons might also be approached upon the subject of model native settlements on parts of their estates which have reached the production stage. Natives of good character might be settled on these lands as tenants.

VII

DISEASE AND ITS TREATMENT

By Sir Wm Macgregor

IN these few lines special stress is laid upon the fact that
one of the greatest—in my humble opinion the most
significant and ominous of all—misfortunes that have be-
fallen the Pacific Islanders has been the introduction among
them of not a few of the most serious diseases that afflict
the white man, without at the same time providing the
means of combating them. A striking example of what this
means was furnished by the epidemic of measles that overran
Fiji in 1874-5, to which between a third and a fourth of the
whole population succumbed. The disease was, so to speak,
in new soil, and flourished accordingly. The psychical effect
was also an important factor in the epidemic, and influenced
the very high rate of mortality; while at the same time the
vitality of those that recovered was lowered. Hardly less
remarkable was the severity of the various forms of venereal
disease, and of dysentery, diseases that, differently from the
epidemic of measles, assumed endemic form and became
domesticated.

Now, the great mortality reported in the press as having
occurred in some of the Pacific Islands from the world-wide
epidemic of influenza, directs in a special manner our attention to the general question of epidemic and other diseases
among the islanders. The subject could be considered from
the point of view of the introduction of disease; and from
that of dealing with diseases actually existing, whether
domesticated or of recent introduction. If the German

possessions in the Western Pacific are, as should be the case, put under the administration of Australia and New Zealand, the introduction of diseases new to the islanders may best be left to those Dominions, where the principles and practice of an efficient quarantine are well understood and carried out. In Australia quarantine safeguards were established on a firm and scientific basis many years ago, chiefly on the initiative of the Hon. Sir Charles Mackellar, then Medical Adviser of the Government of New South Wales.

But the strictest quarantine may fail; and in any case there remains the great and serious question of the diseases already domesticated in the islands, which of themselves, unless at an early date means are provided to minimise their effects, will before long reduce the inhabitants of many of the islands to the verge of extinction. There are cases on record where islanders returning home from a term of years on sugar plantations, have brought with them dysentery that has in one epidemic killed half of the inhabitants.

Of the women and girls that were recruited from the islands for plantation work, few or none went back home without venereal disease of some kind. In one case itch was introduced by a consignment of old clothes—among which figured not a few cast-off police uniforms—and that disease, being entirely new to the natives, assumed quite a serious form, but fortunately did not extend to tribes that wore no clothes. In certain places in the Pacific malarial fevers are not known, while in others they assume the worst form. Ophthalmia, bronchitis, pneumonia, and skin diseases are common. These and other diseases not enumerated make serious inroads on the island population.

Can any practical measures be taken to alleviate this state of matters, bearing in mind the improbability that any form of administration will be able, for financial reasons, to provide, except in very rare cases, a staff of qualified medical practitioners sufficient to meet all requirements?

There can be no doubt that much could, and therefore should be done.

I would most earnestly urge on all Christian Missions at work in the Pacific Islands to have every missionary and teacher, white or coloured, man or woman, put through a course of medical instruction that would enable them to alleviate and mitigate the maladies that now menace the different races of the islanders.

This would be nothing new in missionary work. Indeed, it would only be following the practice of the Founder of our religion, as told to us in each one of the synoptic gospels. The first Christian mission sent out had a double purpose: to preach the approach of the Kingdom, and to cure all infirmities. We know that long before the advent of Christianity, medicine was a sacred art, intimately associated with religion. And we are shown, as for example in Harnack's *Verbreitung des Christentums*, that the Fathers of the primitive church studied and practised medicine.

Many years ago, when it was clear that the Fijian race was losing in number and that the treasury of the Colony could not afford a sufficient staff of qualified medical officers, a scheme was submitted to the Governor, Sir William Des Voeux, and sanctioned by him, whereby some ten or twelve approved students from the Methodist missionary colleges should receive a systematic course of instruction in medicine, and that they should then be appointed to their respective provinces as "Native Medical Practitioners." Their training was entrusted chiefly to Dr Glanvill Corney, I.S.O., who from 1888 to 1908 was Chief Medical Officer of the Colony. How far this scheme was successful may be gathered from the following note by Dr Corney. What is stated therein demonstrates the capacity of the Pacific islander to learn and to practise what is urged above.

"In 1885 the Government of Fiji invited the chiefs to send forward eight or ten young men of proved intelligence, and of good character and family, with a view to their being given a course of instruction in the rudiments of human anatomy and physiology, supplemented by suitable teaching in the wards of the Colonial Hospital, with practice in minor surgery and domestic medicine. The proposal met with a willing response, almost every province contributing at least one student; and these were housed near the Colonial Hospital, where they received technical and disciplinary training from the medical officers and the matron during a term of three years each. Particular attention was paid to such ailments as pneumonia, bronchitis, dysentery, conjunctivitis, and other diseases to which the natives are specially prone, and to the methods for arresting bleeding. General sanitation, both public and individual, and prophylaxis were, of course, included.

In course of time the most promising and careful of these students became useful adjuncts to the labours of the District Medical Officers; and even in parts of the islands out of reach of the latter. As a measure of their ability and precision it may be mentioned that three became in rotation dispensers and anaesthetists at the Hospital, and one of these served with unvarying success for more than a dozen years. Before very long their number reached fifty. Incompetent and otherwise undesirable candidates were generally detected and eliminated from the class long before entering upon a third year of study; but, when the sounder ones had completed the full term, they were subjected to a stiffish examination, written, oral, and practical, and those that passed satisfactorily were awarded a Certificate to that effect. They were then appointed to a provincial post, at first under the supervision of a European Medical Officer, but by degrees their usefulness was availed of, as I have said, for the benefit of the native population of remote islands where no European medical officer was ordinarily within reach, and after some natural hesitation and an occasional rebuff on the part of a biassed and ignorant people, they became greatly appreciated, and no province deemed itself properly equipped without one or more of them, so that the total number of these "Native Practitioners," as they were officially called, has been maintained, and remains at present at more than fifty, year after year.

More recently—1906 or 1907—a class of native women for training as midwives, with particular reference to antisepsis, has been instituted at the hospital under the supervision of the Matron; and many of her pupils have become very popular in the communities amongst whom they work. The course is necessarily much shorter than three years; I believe it is now limited to six months, but something depends upon the number of deliveries available for them to be present at."

When I opened the School for Tropical Medicine at Townsville a few years ago, the superintendent informed me that he would be most happy to receive and instruct European missionaries in tropical medicine on terms exceptionally favourable to them. I have no doubt that the same facilities would be extended to the coloured missionary or teacher.

Then again, one or two duly qualified medical missionaries in each mission could train, or partially train, the coloured or native staff of teachers, who could perhaps have part of their instruction in such matters as anatomy at Townsville, Fiji, or elsewhere.

No doubt assistance would be given by the Federal Government of Australia, and by the Government of New Zealand, who would probably supply such medicines and medical outfit as would be required for the medical missionary.

Valuable information and guidance could be obtained from

the experience gained in Fiji in regard to tuition and general outfit.

That such a training as that outlined above would add to the status and influence of the missionary and teacher cannot be doubted. We see it in the New Testament; and it has been proved many times in the Pacific. Dr Paton, for example, relates how some cures he effected on Tanna saved his own life when in grave danger.

VIII

THE PSYCHOLOGICAL FACTOR

By W. H. R. RIVERS

THE papers by members of the Melanesian Mission and other workers in Melanesia published in this book show conclusively that this great archipelago is undergoing a process of depopulation. In some parts the decline is taking place so rapidly that at no distant date the islands will wholly lose their native inhabitants unless something is done to stay its progress. I propose to begin my contribution to this volume by recounting some facts concerning this dying out of the people noted by myself during visits to Melanesia in 1908 and 1914.

In the New Hebrides the loss of native population is especially great and is progressing rapidly. Not long ago Fate, or Sandwich Island, had a considerable population in which, as usual in Melanesia, it was possible to distinguish between the bush-people and those living near the coast. Now the bush-people have wholly disappeared and the few survivors of the coastal districts have left the main island and live on one or other of the small islands, such as Eretap and Erekor, which fringe its coasts. In the island of Epi further north, the numbers of the people are said to be rapidly declining. Still farther north the shores of the island of Aore are strewn with sherds of pottery which show the former presence of a population of considerable size; now just three inhabitants survive. In Espiritu Santo, usually known as Santo, the largest island of the New Hebrides, the inhabitants of several villages on the west coast have entirely disappeared and their places have been taken by a few wretched people who have moved down from the interior. The little island of Tangoa was formerly the site of three villages, each of which must have been a community of considerable size, for the people are said to have had different dialects. Now all the people of the island live in one small village. At the southern end of Santo the people of Vulua twenty years ago numbered at least 200 according to the estimate of the Rev. F. G. Bowie, the missionary of the district. Now there is only a miserable handful of people, herded together in one village with hardly any children, and they will soon be altogether extinct.

In the Banks and Torres Islands to the north of the New Hebrides the decrease in numbers has been very great. According to a recent estimate of the Rev. R. Godfrey the population of these islands has been reduced by at least one half during the last twenty years. Another member of the Melanesian Mission, the Rev. R. E. Tempest, gives the following figures showing the decrease during the last two or three years:

	1917	1918	1920
Mota	384	—	315
Motalava (Motlav)	697	—	568
Merelava (Merlav)...	—	506	467
Gaua (Santa Maria) 7 villages ...	—	229	215
Ureparapara ...	—	169	150

The rapid decrease is ascribed by Mr Tempest to the inhabitants having been recruited to work in the plantations, chiefly of Espiritu Santo.

In the Santa Cruz group, large islands which are said to have been well peopled are now uninhabited, the decline here having been especially great during the last few years. In the Solomon Islands, the tale is less pitiful, but here also the population of many islands is diminishing so rapidly that unless something is done to stay the decline, it will soon share the fate which has already overtaken so many parts of the New Hebrides.

The Rev. C. E. Fox of the Melanesian Mission has given a striking picture of the decrease of population in San Cristoval in the Solomons. The Spaniards in 1546[1] spoke of the large population of the island. At Wango in 1887 H. B. Guppy[2] estimated the population at about 500; now there are less than 100. From one hill-top Mr Fox was shown the sites of forty-six once flourishing villages of which only three are now inhabited.

Since my visit to Melanesia in 1914 the archipelago has been visited by the severe epidemic of influenza which, here as elsewhere in the Pacific, has done much to hasten the process by which the people of Oceania are disappearing.

The rapidity of the decay at the present time has been brought home to myself by two instances which, though of no great value as evidence, may yet be cited in illustration. During a visit in 1908 I gained a large amount of valuable information from two men, fairly young and apparently full of life and vigour, one a Polynesian living in Melanesia, the other a native of the Banks Islands. I looked forward to their help in future visits to their islands, but before I had had time to record the knowledge they had shared with me, I heard that both were dead. In 1914 I was again in Melanesia and obtained from a still younger native a most important account of a district in the island of Ambrim, whose people had been almost entirely uprooted and destroyed by a volcanic catastrophe. Before I have been able to put this fragment of vanishing knowledge upon record, I hear that the witness is already dead, a victim to the scourge of dysentery.

[1] *The Discovery of the Solomon Islands*, London, Hakluyt Soc., 1901.
[2] *The Solomon Islands and their Natives*, London, 1887, p. 57.

Various causes have been given in this volume to account for the dying out of the people, different factors having been stressed by different authors. I propose to attempt a more complete survey of the causes which lead to decrease of population.

Before beginning this survey it will be well to deal briefly with a supposed fact which has frequently been brought forward as a means of accounting for the decrease of the population of Melanesia. It has been supposed that the Melanesians were already a dying people before the European invasion, and that their decline was due to faults inherent in their own culture. In the first place there is no evidence of any value that the people were decreasing in number before the advent of Europeans. Mr Durrad has dealt with this topic in his contribution to this volume and has failed to find such evidence. It may be true that here and there the people already showed signs of diminution on the arrival of the missionaries[1]. It must be remembered, however, that the people had already been subject for many years to certain European influences, such as that of the sandal-wood hunters, which were far from being of a harmless kind.

When apologists for the effects of their own civilisation give reasons for the supposed original decadence, these often bear their own refutation on the face. Thus, one writer blames the heathen custom of polygamy, but in the same paragraph states that the practice is confined to the few. As if a custom confined to the few could ever be the cause of the dying out of a whole people. As a matter of fact, the polygamy of Melanesia is very different from that of Africa,

---

[1] In some cases this decrease in early times is almost certain. Thus, there is little doubt that the northern end of Ysabel in the Solomons was decimated by the activity of the head-hunters of Ruviana and Eddystone, but this decrease was purely local and had no appreciable influence on the general population of Melanesia.

being so exceptional and the number of wives so small as
to have no appreciable influence upon the people, whether
for good or evil.

Another cause which has been put forward is the special
kind of consanguineous union known as the cross-cousin
marriage. This is a marriage between the children of a
brother and sister which takes place habitually, while marriage between the children of two brothers or of two sisters
is strictly forbidden. This marriage is orthodox in several
parts of Melanesia and is especially frequent and important
in Fiji. This subject was fully investigated by the Commission which more than twenty years ago inquired into the
decrease of the native population of Fiji. In their *Report*[1],
which forms a storehouse of most valuable facts concerning
the topics of this book, it is shown conclusively that this
factor had not contributed towards Fijian decadence, but
rather that these consanguineous marriages were more
fruitful than marriage between wholly unrelated persons.

I shall deal presently with native customs in relation to
our subject and hope to show that it is rather the indiscri-
minate and undiscriminating interference with them which
stands forth prominently among the causes of decay.

I can now consider the conditions to which real efficacy
in the process of destruction can be assigned. In studying
this subject the first point to bear in mind is the double
character of the factors upon which fluctuation of population
depends, a double character which holds good of Melanesia
as of more civilised parts of the world. Diminution of population may be due to increase of the death-rate or to decrease
of the birth-rate, or to both combined. I can bring forward
evidence to show that both factors have been active in

---

[1] *Report of the Commission appointed to inquire into the Decrease
of the Native Population (Colony of Fiji)*, Suva, 1896.

Melanesia. I will begin with the conditions which have affected the death-rate.

In a subject in which we can find little on which to pride ourselves, it is satisfactory to be able to exclude one cause of depopulation which has contributed in no small measure to the disappearance of native races in other parts of the world. There has been no deliberate attempt to exterminate the people such as has disgraced the history of our relations with regions more suited to European habitation than the sweltering and unhealthy islands of Melanesia. The injurious influences due to European rulers and settlers have been unwitting. Owing to the need for the labour of those accustomed to the tropics, it has always been in the interests of the settlers that the native population shall be alive and healthy. In so far as native decay is due to European influence we have to lay the blame on ignorance and lack of foresight, not on any deliberate wish to destroy.

In considering the death of a people as of an individual, it is natural to think first of disease. Disease is the name we give to a group of processes by which the size of a population is adjusted so as to enable it best to utilise the available means of subsistence. Before the arrival of Europeans, Melanesia had its own diseases, by means of which Nature helped to keep the population within bounds. Everything goes to show that the population of Melanesia was well within the limits which the country was capable of supporting, but it is not so certain that it was far within this capacity in relation to the very simple means the people possessed for exploiting its resources. So far as we can tell, there had been set up a state of equilibrium between the size of the population and the available resources of the country. Recent knowledge goes to show that the diseases due to infective parasites tend to set up a state of tolerance and habituation which renders a people less prone to succumb to their ravages, and there is no reason to suppose that Melanesia was any exception in this respect. Thus the people are largely habituated to the malaria which certainly existed among them before the coming of European influence.

Into this community thus adapted to the infective agents of their own country, the invaders brought a number of new diseases: measles, dysentery, probably tubercle and influenza, and last but unfortunately far from least potent, venereal disease. These maladies had effects far more severe than those they bring upon ourselves, partly because they found a virgin soil, partly because the native therapeutic ideas were not adapted to the new diseases, so that remedies were often used which actually increased their harmfulness. Many of these introduced diseases are still drawing a large toll on the numbers and energies of the people, the two which seem to be exerting the most steady influence, so far as my observations show, being dysentery and tubercle.

A second group of introduced causes of destruction is composed of what may be called the social poisons, such as alcohol and opium. Though it is possible that the people use tobacco somewhat to excess, the only poison which needs to be considered in Melanesia is alcohol. In certain parts of Melanesia there is no question that it has exerted in the past and is still exerting a most deleterious influence, but it is satisfactory to be able to say that its noxious influence has been reduced to negligible importance in those parts of the archipelago wholly subject to British rule, where it is penal to sell or give alcohol to a native. Alcohol is still, however, potent as a cause of disease and death in the New Hebrides. In those islands there are regulations against the sale of alcohol to natives, but under the present Condominium Government they are not obeyed.

A third direct cause of increase of death-rate is the introduction of fire-arms, by means of which the comparatively harmless warfare of the natives is given a far more deadly turn. This cause is still active to some extent in the New Hebrides owing to breaking of the regulations of the Condominium Government, but fire-arms have never had great importance as an instrument of destruction in Melanesia.

I come to a more serious cause when I consider European influence upon native customs. I begin with one which excites perennial interest whenever native welfare is discussed. Before the advent of Europeans the people of some islands went wholly nude or wore only garments, if they can be so called, which fulfilled neither of the two chief purposes for which the clothing of civilised people is designed. In other parts the native clothing consisted of petticoats, loin-cloths, or other simple garments thoroughly adapted to the necessities of the climate. One of the first results of European influence was the adoption of the clothing of the visitors, and clothes were adopted in such a manner as to accentuate the evils which they necessarily brought with them. The Melanesian is not uncleanly. He bathes frequently, and where he preserves his native mode of clothing, his ablutions are amply sufficient for cleanliness. When he wears European garments, he fails to adopt measures, such as the frequent change of clothing, which then become necessary. He continues to bathe in his clothes, and instead of changing his garments frequently, wears them continuously till they are ragged, and even when new clothing is obtained, it is put over the old.

It is a great mistake, often made, to blame the missionaries for this use of foreign clothing. It is true that its use was directly encouraged by the early missionaries, but this encouragement was unnecessary. To the native, trousers and coats are the distinctive mark of the white man, and nothing short of prohibition could have prevented their use. Where we can now see the missionaries to have been at fault is that they did not recognise the evil of the innovation and set themselves steadily to minimise it. They should have insisted upon attention to the elementary principles of the hygiene which the use of clothes involves.

At the present time the influence of missionaries is steadily directed to this end. Having been privileged to live among missionaries of different schools of thought in Melanesia, I can testify that no subject is more frequently discussed and more thoroughly and anxiously considered than how to lessen the use and injurious influence of European clothing.

Another modification of native custom, which is less widely recognised, but in my experience quite as much in need of consideration at the present time, is housing. The native Melanesian house is usually rain-proof and of good proportions, while owing to its mode of construction it is well ventilated and thoroughly adapted to the climate. Instead of being content with houses of similar construction or with houses of the kind used by Europeans living in other tropical countries, settlers have built houses with thick walls and very imperfect means of ventilation. These have in some cases been copied by the natives, or even built by the missionaries for the use of their followers. Such buildings might have been specially devised for the propagation of tubercle, and if they are allowed to be built will certainly increase the already far too heavy ravages of this disease.

The modifications of housing and clothing which I have just considered touch especially the material side of life. I have now to consider a number of modifications and interferences with native custom which I believe to have been quite as important, if not more important, in the production of native decadence. When Melanesia became subject to Europeans, magistrates and missionaries were sent to rule and direct the lives of the people. They found in existence a number of institutions and customs which were, or seemed to them to be, contrary to the principles of morality. Such customs were usually forbidden without any inquiry into their real nature, without knowledge of the part they took in native life, and without any attempt to discriminate between their good and bad elements. Thus, in the Solomon Islands the rulers stopped the special kind of warfare known as head-hunting, without at all appreciating the vast place it took in the religious and ceremonial lives of the people, without realising the gap it would leave in their daily interests, a blank far more extensive than that due to the mere cessation of a mode of warfare. Again, in Fiji, the custom according to which the men of the community slept apart from the women in a special house, a widespread custom in Melanesia, seemed to the missionaries contrary to the ideals of the Christian family, and the custom was stopped or discouraged without it being realised that the segregation of the sexes formed an effectual check on too free intercourse between them.

In the New Hebrides again, the missionaries put an end to, or where they did not destroy, treated with a barely veiled contempt, a highly complicated organisation arising out of beliefs connected with the cult of dead ancestors. In some cases it was apparent enough that the institution with all its elaborate ceremonial was heathen and prejudiced church attendance, while elsewhere stress was laid on occasional revels and dances which gave opportunity for licence. It was not recognised that in forbidding or discouraging without inquiry, they were destroying institutions which had the most far-reaching ramifications through the social and economical life of the people. I have called attention to this subject elsewhere in an essay on "The Government of Subject Peoples," included in the Cambridge collection of essays entitled *Science and the Nation*[1]. I have there pointed out that if these and similar institutions had been studied before they were destroyed or discouraged, it would have been found possible to discriminate between those features which were noxious and needed repression or amendment, and those which were beneficial to the welfare of the community. Even when their destruction was deemed necessary, something could have been done to replace the social sanctions of which the people were thus deprived. The point I wish to emphasise is that through this unintelligent and undiscriminating action towards native institutions, the people were deprived of nearly all that gave interest to their lives. I have now to suggest that this loss of interest forms one of the reasons, if indeed it be not the most potent of all the reasons, to which the native decadence is due.

It may at first sight seem far-fetched to suppose that such a factor as loss of interest in life could ever produce the dying out of a people, but my own observations have led me to the conclusion that its influence is so great that it can hardly be overrated. I venture therefore to consider it at some length.

When you inquire of those who have lived long in Melanesia concerning the illness and mortality of the natives, you are struck by the frequency of reference to the ease with which the native dies. Over and over again one is told of a native who seemed hale and well until, after a day or two of some apparently trivial illness, he gives up the ghost without any of the signs which among ourselves usually give ample warning of the impending fate. A native who is ill loses

[1] Cambridge Univ. Press, 1917, p. 302.

heart at once. He has no desire to live, and perhaps announces that he is going to die when the onlooker can see no ground for his belief.

The matter becomes more easy to understand if we consider the ease with which the people are killed by magic or as the result of the infraction of a taboo. The evidence is overwhelming that such people as the Melanesians will sicken and die in a few hours or days as the result of the belief that an enemy has chosen them as the victim of his spells, or that they have, wittingly or unwittingly, offended against some religious taboo. If people who are interested in life and do not wish to die can be killed in a few days or even hours by a mere belief, how much more easy it is to understand that a people who have lost all interest in life should become the prey of any morbid agency acting through the body as well as through the mind. It is this evidence of the enormous influence of the mind upon the body among the Melanesians and other lowly peoples that first led me to attach so much importance to loss of interest as the primary cause of their dying out. Once this belief has been formulated, there is seen to be much definite evidence in Melanesia to support it.

Certain islands and districts of Melanesia show a degree of vitality in striking contrast with the rest. These exceptional cases fall into two classes: one includes those islands or parts of islands where the people have so far been fierce and strong enough to withstand European influence. There are still certain parts in Melanesia which as yet the footprint of the white man has not reached, and others where, after successful encounters with punitive expeditions, the people still believe themselves to be a match for the invader. Here the old zest and interest in life persist and the people are still vigorous and abundant.

The other group of peoples who show signs of vitality are those who have adopted Christianity, not merely because it is the religion of the powerful white man, but with a whole-hearted enthusiasm which has given them a renewed interest in life. Here the numbers are increasing after an initial drop. Christianity and the occupations connected with it have given the people a new interest to replace that of their indigenous culture, and with this interest has come the desire to live.

The special point I wish to make in my contribution to this book is that interest in life is the primary factor in the welfare of a people. The new diseases and poisons, the innovations in clothing, housing and feeding, are only the immediate causes of mortality. It is the loss of interest in life underlying these more obvious causes which gives them their potency for evil and allows them to work such ravages upon life and health.

I can pass to the second of the two groups of influences by which a people decline in number, having so far dealt only with those which increase the death-rate. I have now to consider those which produce decline by diminishing the birth-rate and will begin by stating briefly the evidence that this factor has played and is playing a part in the dying out of the Melanesians. This evidence has been gained by a mode of inquiry adopted originally for purely scientific purposes. When in Torres Straits with Dr Haddon twenty-four years ago, I discovered that the people preserved in their memories with great fidelity a full and accurate record of their descent and relationships[1]. It was possible to collect pedigrees so ample in all collateral lines that they could serve as a source of statistical inquiry into such features as

[1] See *Journ. Anthrop. Inst.* 1900, xxx. p. 74; and *Sociological Review*, 1910, iii. p. 1.

the average size of a family, infant mortality, and other subjects which furnish the basis for conclusions concerning fluctuations of population. I have found this interest in genealogy wherever I have worked, and the collection of pedigrees has always formed the basis of my ethnographic inquiries. In Melanesia this instrument shows conclusively that the fall in numbers is due quite as much to decrease of the birth-rate as to increase of the death-rate.

I will begin with the evidence from the Solomon Islands. I have a large collection of pedigrees from two islands of the group, Eddystone Island and Vella Lavella. The result of the analysis of these pedigrees is given in the two following tables, which make it possible to compare, if only in a rough manner, the fertility of the present with that of preceding generations. The tables record in percentages the size of the family, the proportion of childless marriages, and other data for three successive generations. The chief difficulty arose in dealing with the third or present generation, for its marriages evidently include a number which, though childless or with only a small family at present, may be expected to result in offspring, or more offspring, in time. A certain number of marriages, viz. 9·1 per cent. of this generation were therefore set aside as doubtful, as shown in the eighth column of the table. It is possible that a certain number of the marriages included in the childless category of the fourth column may also become fruitful, and there may also be a slight increase in the figures recording the number of children per marriage. Thus, though the record of childless marriages only includes cases where it seemed safe to assume that the marriage would be permanently sterile, the figure is probably somewhat larger than it would be if the record could be taken ten years hence. Similarly, the figures giving the size of the family in this generation would also show some increase.

The division into generations was necessarily rough, but was effected before any attempt was made to estimate fertility. The objections which I have considered do not apply

Table I. Eddystone Island.

Generation	Total No. of marriages	Total No. of children	Childless marriages in %	Marriages with			Number of children doubtful	Children who died young in %	
				1 or 2 children	3 to 5 children	6 or more children		M	F
I	207	447	19·4	43·5	32·8	4·3	—	6·4	4·5
II	295	379	46·1	29·0	18·9	3·3	2·7	18·5	8·1
III	110	72	52·7	32·7	5·5	0	9·1	31·1	14·8

Table II. Vella Lavella.

Generation	Total No. of marriages	Total No. of children	Childless marriages in %	Marriages with			No. of children doubtful	Children who died young	
				1 or 2 children	3 to 5 children	6 or more children		M	F
I	116	279	12·1	4·2	41·4	4·3	—	1·7	2·7
II	209	297	35·4	37·8	21·1	1·4	4·3	6·3	3·7
III	57	15	71·9	22·8	0	0	5·3	25·0	28·6

to the comparison of the two earlier generations, though there is the possibility that persons of the earlier generation may have been altogether omitted from the pedigrees because, owing to the absence of children, they were not of social importance, so that their existence had been forgotten. It is possible that this factor may have come into action to some extent in the pedigrees from Vella Lavella, but it is improbable that it has had any influence on the Eddystone figures, for these were collected from several sources and verified in many ways. It is possible that persons who failed to marry may have been omitted, but improbable that persons who married would have escaped record.

The Eddystone figures are more satisfactory than those of Vella Lavella in many respects, for they are based on a fairly complete genealogical record of the whole population of the island, whereas the pedigrees of Vella Lavella are only samples collected here and there from a population very much larger than that of Eddystone.

The Eddystone figures show decisively how great has been the influence of some factor or factors leading to decrease in the size of the family. Childless marriages increased in frequency from 19·4 to 46·1 per cent. in passing from the first to the second generation. As I have already mentioned the increase to 52·7 per cent. in the present generation may possibly be illusory owing to certain families being still incomplete, but this factor cannot possibly explain the great increase in the number of childless marriages in the earlier generation. Equally striking are the figures showing the total number of children recorded for each generation in the pedigrees. Whereas two generations ago, 207 marriages produced 447 children, or well over two children per marriage, the figures for the following generation were 379 children from 295 marriages or an average of less than a child and a half per marriage. In the present generation the record is even worse, only 72 children having been born from 110 marriages, or less than one child per marriage. This figure may be expected, however, to become somewhat larger when recent marriages have produced their full effect upon the population.

The figures recording the size of the family are equally depressing. They show a striking decrease in the number of families of more than five. The last two columns give the infant mortality of the two sexes. It is a question whether children who died young may not have been in many cases forgotten in the case of the earliest generation and therefore omitted when the pedigrees were collected, and in this case the increase in infant mortality would not be as great as represented in the table. It will be noted that the mortality is definitely greater in the case of male children, but here again there is the possibility that male children who died young would be remembered better and that some female children who died in infancy may have been forgotten and therefore omitted.

The record of the island of Vella Lavella in the Solomons is similar in its nature but shows an even more serious decrease of fertility. As I have already mentioned, however, the record is less trustworthy. The island is much larger than Eddystone and the figures given in the table are derived from random samples taken from various villages of the coast. The record differs from that of Eddystone in that the number of childless marriages has shown a progressive increase to the present day, but as I did not know the people and their circumstances as I knew them in Eddystone no great significance should be attached to the figure for the present generation. It is significant, however, that the proportion of childless marriages two generations ago, viz. 12·1 per cent., does not differ greatly from the Eddystone figure.

Especially noteworthy is the total disappearance of families of more than two children in the present generation of Vella Lavella. Equally striking is the great diminution in the total number of children in this generation, the names of only fifteen children from marriages of this generation being recorded.

The two islands which show this striking fall in birth-rate are of especial interest in that in them, and especially in Eddystone, the chief factors to which the dying out of peoples is usually ascribed are absent. In Eddystone, about which a residence of several months enables me to speak with confidence, there is no record of any very severe epidemics. Tubercle and dysentery, the two most deadly diseases in Melanesia, do not appear to be, or to have been, especially active; and though both the chief forms of venereal disease exist in the island, they do not seem to have done any great amount of mischief. The island has never had a white missionary; the people still wear their native dress and live in houses of native build. Alcohol is little known and other poisons not at all, while any effect of fire-arms on mortality is negligible. Few of the people have left the island as labour or for any other reason. All the factors to which other writers in this book ascribe the decrease of the population of Melanesia are practically absent, and yet we have a striking diminution of population, due in the main to decrease of the birth-rate.

If now we pass from material to mental factors, the decrease in the birth-rate becomes easier to understand. No one could be long in Eddystone without recognising how great is the people's lack of interest in life and to what an extent the zest has gone out of their lives. This lack of interest is largely due to the abolition of head-hunting by the British Government. This practice formed the centre of a social and religious institution which took an all-pervading part in the lives of the people. The heads sought in the head-hunting expeditions were needed in order to propitiate the ancestral ghosts on such occasions as building a new house for a chief or making a new canoe, while they were also offered in sacrifice at the funeral of a chief. Moreover, head-hunting was not only necessary for the due performance of the religious rites of the people, but it stood in the closest relation to pursuits of an economic kind. The actual head-hunting expedition only lasted a few weeks, and the actual fighting often only a few hours, but this was only the culminating point of a process lasting over years. It was the rule that new canoes should be made for an expedition to obtain heads, and the manufacture of these meant work of an interesting kind lasting certainly for many months, probably for years. The process of canoe-building was accompanied throughout by rites and feasts which not only excited the liveliest interest but also acted as stimuli to various activities of horticulture and pig-breeding. As the date fixed for the expedition approached other rites and feasts were held, and these were still more frequent and on a larger scale after the return of a successful expedition. In stopping the practice of head-hunting the rulers from an alien culture were abolishing an institution which had its roots in the religion of the people and spread its branches throughout nearly every aspect of their culture, and by this action they deprived the people of the greater part of their interest in life, while at the same time they undermined the religion of the people without any attempt to put another in its place.

The other region of Melanesia where, through the application of the genealogical method, I am able to demonstrate the existence of a greatly lowered birth-rate is the New Hebrides. During my visit to that group in 1914 I did not stay in any one place long enough to collect a full genealogical record, as in Eddystone, but I obtained sample pedigrees in various islands which show clearly a state of affairs similar to that of the Solomons. I have already mentioned the people of Vulua in Espiritu Santo as an example of a people who have almost disappeared, and a pedigree obtained from one of the survivors well illustrates the chief factor to which their disappearance is due. About eighty years ago, when Santo was hardly touched by outside influences, a man of Vulua named Rathati married. He had four children whose marriages gave Rathati fifteen grandchildren, of whom my informant, a man verging towards middle age, was the sole survivor. Of the fifteen grandchildren of Rathati ten grew to adult age and married, but only two of these unions produced offspring: in one case a boy who died in infancy, while in the other case there were three children. All three of these children, the only great-grandchildren of Rathati, reached adult age and married, but none had offspring, so that a family which was once rapidly growing in numbers is now closing its career with a monotonous record of sterile marriages.

Another pedigree shows a man of Tasariki in Santo to have had five children whose marriages produced nine grandchildren. Six of these grandchildren married, but only two have been fruitful and in each of these cases the family is limited to one. Childless marriages are of frequent occurrence in other pedigrees collected in the New Hebrides, showing that there, as in the Solomons, lowered birth-rate must rank with enhanced death-rate as an important factor in the disappearance of the people.

I need only consider here very briefly the agencies to which this fall in birth-rate is due. It is well known that certain forms of venereal disease will produce sterility, and it is noteworthy that the dying out of the people of Vulua is ascribed by their neighbours to the ravages of this disease brought by returning labourers from Queensland. There is little doubt, however, that if we take Melanesia as a whole, causes of this kind are trivial or of slight importance as compared with voluntary restriction. Throughout Melanesia the people are acquainted with various means of producing abortion and also practise measures which they believe to prevent conception, and processes of this kind almost certainly form the main agencies in lowering the birth-rate. We have here only another effect of the loss of interest in life which I have held to be so potent in enhancing mortality. The people say themselves: "Why should we bring children into the world only to work for the white man?" Measures which, before the coming of the European, were used chiefly to prevent illegitimacy have become the instrument of racial suicide.

It is satisfactory that before I leave this subject I am able to point to a brighter side. I have already said that in certain parts of Melanesia the downward movement has been arrested and that the people now show signs of growth. I mentioned also that this was occurring especially in islands where the people have really taken to their hearts the lessons of their Christian teachers. I collected pedigrees from several Christian islands and they tell a tale vastly different from the miserable record of Vulua. A man of Makura named Masosopo, who married about seventy years ago, had three children and nine grandchildren, and there are already fourteen great-grandchildren, with a prospect of more to come, a striking contrast with the impending disappearance of the Vulua family. A couple who married about the same time in Nguna now have twenty-three descendants living and thriving, while in other islands I have records of families from eight to ten in number.

The teachings of the missionaries concerning the evils of racial suicide may possibly have contributed in some degree to this recovery, though I doubt whether in general they have been aware of the part which voluntary restriction has taken. I believe that their influence has lain much more in the fact that the religion they have taught has given the people a renewed interest in life which has again made it worth while to bring children into the world.

Until now I have said nothing of a cause of depopulation which has been especially active in Melanesia. The causes I have so far considered have been treated under two headings, according as they have enhanced the death-rate or lowered the birth-rate. The labour-traffic which I have now to consider is more complex and involves both of these factors.

In dealing with this cause of depopulation it is well that it is possible to begin by distinguishing between the traffic as it was and as it is. It would be difficult to exaggerate the evil influence of the process by which the natives of Melanesia were taken to Australia and elsewhere to labour for the white man. It forms one of the blackest of civilisation's crimes. Not least among its evils was the manner of its ending, when large numbers of people who had learnt by many years' experience to adapt themselves to civilised ways were, in the process of so-called repatriation, thrust back into savagery without help of any kind. The misery thus caused and the resulting disaffection not only underlie most of the open troubles in the recent history of Melanesia, but by the production of a state of helplessness and hopelessness have contributed as much as any other factors to the decline of the population.

I must not, however, dwell on the crimes and mistakes of the past. Our object in this book is to call attention to existing evils in the hope that they may be remedied before it is too late. At the present time Melanesians are only recruited as labourers to work within the confines of Melanesia, and both the recruitment and the conditions of labour are subject to Government control. Its grosser evils have been removed, at any rate in those parts of Melanesia which are wholly governed by Great Britain, though it would appear that there are still very grave defects in those parts of Melanesia under the control of the Condominium Government. But however closely and wisely the traffic is controlled, the removal from their own homes of the younger men, and still more of the younger women, of a declining population is not a factor which can tend to arrest the decline or convert it into a movement in the opposite direction. Even in its improved form, and limited to Melanesia though it be, the labour traffic continues to act as a cause of depopulation. It acts directly by taking men and women away from their homes when they should be marrying and producing children, while other evils are that, as at present conducted, the traffic tends to spread disease and to undermine an influence which I believe to be at the present time the most potent for good in Melanesia, the work of the missionaries. Moreover, the use of natives as labourers on plantations fails to give that interest in life which, as I have tried to show, forms the most essential factor in maintaining the health of a people.

Thus far in this contribution I have been dealing with the causes to which the dying out of the Melanesian people must be ascribed. To use medical language suitable to such a state of affairs as that recorded in this volume, I have been attempting to make a diagnosis. It is now time to turn to treatment and inquire what can be done to arrest the decline and make the Melanesians again a thriving and vigorous people. If I am right in my diagnosis that the chief cause of decline is lack of interest, it is not difficult to see the general lines upon which successful treatment must be based.

I shall pass, therefore, with a mere mention those lines
of treatment, dictated by the ordinary principles of hygiene,
by means of which faults of clothing, housing and feeding
may be remedied, and shall confine my attention to the
factor which I believe to stand first and foremost among the
causes of the dying out of the Melanesian—the loss of interest in life from which at present he is suffering.

The main problem of treatment is how far it is possible
to restore the old interests, or maintain them where they
have not yet been destroyed, and how far they must be
replaced by others. As I have already mentioned, there are
still certain parts of Melanesia where the old life still persists
with but little change. It would be an interesting experiment to see how far it is possible in these cases to maintain
the old interests and make them the foundation on which
to build a culture which would not conflict with the ethical
and social ideals of the people who have come to be their
rulers.

To most of the writers in this volume, and probably to
most of its readers, such an experiment would not appeal,
for it is naturally to the total replacement of the old religious
interests by new that they will look for the remedy. It may
be instructive, however, to consider for a moment how far
it would be possible to modify the old customs and institutions of the people; to preserve enough to maintain interest
while removing all those features which conflict with the
ideals of modern civilisation. For this purpose I will take
an extreme case and consider whether it would have been
possible to have modified such a practice as the head-
hunting of the Solomons. At first sight it might seem a
hopeless task, and so it would be if one attended only to the
outward practice obvious to the European observer and
ignored the meaning which the institution of head-hunting

bears to those who practice it. If we turn to this inner meaning, the case becomes less difficult. The essential motive for the head-hunting of Melanesia is the belief that on various important occasions, and especially on occasions connected with the chiefs, a human head is necessary as an offering to the ancestral ghosts. There is little doubt that the custom is a relic of an earlier practice of human sacrifice, and the head-hunting of the Solomons was but little removed from this, for till recently it was the custom to bring home from expeditions captives who were killed when some important ceremony created the need for a head. In other parts of the world there is reason to believe that, where human beings were formerly sacrificed, the place of the human victim has been taken by an animal, and even that the place of a human head has been taken by that of an animal. I have no doubt that it would have been possible to effect such a substitution in the Solomons, that officials with the necessary knowledge of native custom and belief, and with some degree of sympathy with them, could have brought about such a substitution and thus avoided the loss of life and money which has accompanied the suppression of head-hunting in the Solomons. At the same time they would have kept up the interest of the people in their native institutions until such time as the march of events produced new interests, including new religious interests, connected with the culture which was being brought to bear upon their lives.

The substitution of the head of a pig for that of a human being would not, however, wholly solve the problem. I have already mentioned that the chief stimulus to the making of canoes in Eddystone Island came out of the practice of head-hunting. The substitution of a porcine for a human head, while satisfying many of the ceremonial needs, would leave no motive for the manufacture of new canoes and the

maintenance of this industry. Here it would be necessary
to provide some new motive for the making of canoes. This
might be found in the introduction of canoe races as elements
in the ceremonial connected with the ancestral offerings,
while to this might be added economic motives connected
with fishing or trade. It is probable that in such a process
of substitution the native canoe would be displaced by the
boat of European build, but much as this would be regretted
by the anthropologist or the artist, this form of craft would
be probably fully as efficacious in maintaining interest and
zest in life and would thus contribute to the purpose which
the writers of this volume have before them. Only, it is
essential that the change should grow naturally out of native
institutions and should not be forced upon the people without their consent and without any attempt to rouse their
interest.

In this brief sketch of the lines upon which native customs
might be modified so as to bring them into harmony with
European culture I have already mentioned incidentally the
introduction of new economic interests. I must now consider
this subject more explicitly. In former days the chief need
of the people outside their own island or district was for
certain weapons and for kinds of food which did not flourish
at home. Here it is noteworthy that the need for food from
without was often connected with religion. Thus, one of the
chief reasons why the people of Eddystone went elsewhere
for the taro which did not flourish in their own island was
its inclusion among the foods which should be used in certain
ceremonial feasts, an example which shows how motives due
to trade and the interest arising therefrom are often closely
connected with religion. If religious interest flags, other interests, which might at first sight seem wholly devoid of any
connection with it, will flag also.

At the present time the natives of Melanesia have acquired certain new needs through their contact with European influence, especially the need for tobacco and calico, while in many parts external influence has produced a liking for rice and other introduced foods which have had a most destructive influence on native horticulture. In order to obtain the articles thus needed the Melanesian has to do a certain amount of work, chiefly that involved in the collection and drying of coconuts to make copra. This takes little of his time and has in it little or nothing to arouse interest.

One of the chief needs of Melanesia is that the native shall be given a real interest in the economic development of his country. The Melanesian is a keen trader and there are cases in the New Hebrides in which he has shown much ability when he has entered as an ordinary trader into competition with the European. There is no question that if he were given a fair chance, he could take an important part in any organisation which had as its object the encouragement of native industry. Until recently the missionary societies of Melanesia have made no attempt at industrial development, either to encourage the old industries or to introduce new, and the Government has done even less in this direction. The only neighbouring region of Oceania where any progress in this direction has been made is in Torres Straits, where "The Papuan Industries Company" has endeavoured to give to the natives that share in the management of the industries of their country which is the best means of bringing back the old interest and zest in life. In other parts of the world, and pre-eminently in West Africa, such movements have had the most striking success and there is no reason why the success should not be as great in Melanesia.

It is doubtful, however, whether the modification of native custom and the replacement of old economic interests by new will be sufficient to allow the Melanesian to enter once more upon an upward course of progress. The old life of the people was permeated through and through by interests of a religious kind, based on a profound belief in continued existence after death and in the influence of the dead upon the welfare of the living. Experience has amply shown that Christianity is capable of giving the people an interest in life which can take the place of that due to their indigenous religion. Even if it were thought desirable to maintain the native religion in a modified form, it is highly improbable that there will be found people of our own culture sufficiently self-sacrificing to guide the progress of the people in the way which comes so naturally to the missionaries of the Christian religion. But if this religion is to help in the restoration of the material welfare of the people it is essential that its leaders shall recognise the difficulties which beset their path and should have a definite policy in connection with these difficulties.

Few things have done more harm in the past than the absence of such a policy and the consequent doubt and uncertainty concerning the attitude towards native institutions. Where one missionary has seen nothing but the work of the devil in some native institution and has willed its complete destruction, another, perhaps even of the same Mission, has seen in it a means of preparing the ground for the truth and has, to some extent at least, encouraged its activities. Faced with this difference of attitude the native has in his doubt been led into dissimulation. He has tried to combine the old and the new without discrimination and without the guidance which should have come from those whose business it should be to understand the religious practices they were displacing. If a new gospel is to be taken with success to such a people as the Melanesian, it is essential

that the indigenous point of view shall be understood and
that the misunderstanding to which the new views are inevitably subject shall be appreciated. Even if it were decided
utterly to destroy the old religion there is no way in which
these difficulties can be met so successfully as by a study of
the old religion and of the mental attitude upon which the
old religious practices rested, for this attitude must inevitably influence the reception of the new religion. If, on
the other hand, it be decided to preserve such elements
of the old religion as are not in conflict with the new, this
study is even more essential. How can it be possible to
decide whether a native practice shall be preserved unless
the nature of the practice is thoroughly understood and its
relations with other aspects of the native culture realised[1]?
Whatever the policy adopted towards the indigenous religion, it is of the utmost importance that this religion shall
be understood and that, even if no concerted effort to study
native religions is made, attempts in this direction made by
individual missionaries shall be encouraged.

Another question of policy which must be faced concerns
the attitude which the missionary is to take towards economic development. I have already pointed out the close
relation between religion and economics in the indigenous
society of Melanesia. Such institutions as the *Sukwe* of the
Banks Islands[2] or the ancestor-cult of the Solomons stand
in the closest relation to economic needs and cannot be modified or abolished without producing far-reaching changes in
the social and economic life of the people. These are only
individual instances of a feature of early forms of human

[1] I have dealt with this subject in its relation to government in
the paper already quoted, "The Government of Subject Peoples,"
published in *Science and the Nation*, Cambridge Univ. Press, 1917,
p. 302.

[2] See *History of Melanesian Society*, Cambridge, 1914, I. p. 140.

culture according to which they show a far greater interdependence of different aspects of social life than exists
among ourselves. Even in our own society a new law in-
tended by legislators to act upon some one branch of social
life often produces changes of a far-reaching kind on other
aspects which were wholly unforeseen when the law was
passed. Such interdependence is even greater in such simple
societies as those of Melanesia, and it is very unlikely that
this interdependence will cease with the introduction of new
customs from without. The economic life of the people of
Melanesia is being profoundly modified by external influence,
but it is doubtful whether the close relation between economic and religious interests will disappear. It is essential
that the missionary shall face this problem and make up his
mind concerning the attitude he is going to adopt towards
the economic life of the people. In the past many of the best
missionaries of all denominations have set their faces against
mixing economic problems with their religion. It has seemed
to them that in so doing the spiritual side of religion must
inevitably suffer, and no one who has had the opportunity
of observing sporadic examples of the mixture can fail to
sympathise with them. It must be recognised, however, that
there is a problem and that it is in urgent need of settlement.
If, as seems natural, economic development is made the
business of the civil power, while the missionary occupies
himself wholly with religion, there will be endless opportunities for conflict. The best course is one in which Government and missionary societies join in common council to
decide how they can avert the disappearance of the Melanesian. The lesson of this article is that something must be
done, and done quickly, to give him that renewed interest
in life to which the health of peoples is mainly due.

INDEX

For EU product safety concerns, contact us at Calle de José Abascal, 56–1°,
28003 Madrid, Spain or eugpsr@cambridge.org.

www.ingramcontent.com/pod-product-compliance
Ingram Content Group UK Ltd.
Pitfield, Milton Keynes, MK11 3LW, UK
UKHW020313140625
459647UK00018B/1859